Call Sign Rustic

The Secret Air
War over
Cambodia,
1970–1973

CALL SIGN
RUSTIC

Richard
Wood

SMITHSONIAN INSTITUTION PRESS
Washington and London

Production editor: Robert A. Poarch
Designer: Janice Wheeler

Library of Congress Cataloging-in-Publication Data
Wood, Richard, 1931–
    Call sign Rustic : the secret air war over Cambodia, 1970–1973 / Richard Wood ; foreword by
Mark Berent.
        p.   cm.
    Includes bibliographical references and index.
    ISBN 1-58834-049-X
    1.   Cambodia—History—Civil War, 1970–1975—Aerial operations, American.
2.   Vietnamese Conflict, 1961–1975—Campaigns—Laos. 3.   Vietnamese Conflict, 1961–1975—
Aerial operations, American.   I. Title.
    DS554.8 .W66 2002
    959.704′3—dc21   2002019198

British Library Cataloguing-in-Publication Data is available
Manufactured in the United States of America

07 06 05 04 03 02   5 4 3 2 1

♾ The paper used in this publication meets the minimum requirements of the American National
Standard for Information Sciences—Permanence of Paper for Printed Library Materials ANSI
Z39.48-1984.

This book is dedicated to the Rustics killed in action in the air war in Cambodia

1st Lt. Garrett Edward Eddy, O-2 pilot, born December 22, 1944, killed in action north of Tang Kouk, Cambodia, October 1, 1970

1st Lt. Michael Stephen Vrablick, O-2 pilot, born July 8, 1946, killed in action north of Tang Kouk, Cambodia, October 1, 1970

1st Lt. Joseph Gambino Jr, OV-10 pilot, born July 4, 1949, killed in action south of Kompong Thom, Cambodia, April 7, 1973

This book is also dedicated to the many Cambodian friends of the Rustics who lost their lives in the defense of their country

When good men die, their goodness does not perish, but lives though they are gone. —Euripides

Contents

Foreword

Several decades have passed since I returned from my assignment at the American Embassy in Phnom Penh, Cambodia. I'm filled with so many memories; some sweet, some bitter, but all of them so intense I can re-create any given moment in my mind. The most vivid memories spring from the events in the spring and summer of 1973, toward the end of American airpower involvement.

In that year we had the Vietnam War in miniature going on in Cambodia. It was the same old formula: American government promises, fighting escalates, American government pulls out. Initially the American commitment was quite marginal in a country delighted to have us help in their fight against the communist aggressor. They welcomed us as if we were the cavalry riding to the rescue in a scene from an old John Wayne movie. That attitude, of the fighting Cambodians, the ones truly dedicated to protecting their country, made us feel we could, unlike in South Vietnam, accomplish something positive. We Americans in the embassy, some of us anyhow, felt excited in that we could apply the bitter lessons learned in South Vietnam to the current situation. We honestly felt we could make a difference. Almost all of us had at least one combat tour in Vietnam and we had no difficulty remembering how it was.

In January of 1973, much to Ho Chi Minh's delight, a cowardly Congress stopped American combat in Vietnam. However, the Nixon-Kissinger duo permitted full American air support to continue in Cambodia until August 15, 1973. This meant that B-52 and FB-111 bombers were available around the clock, AC-130 Spectre gunships along with Vietnamese gunships were available during the night, and more than two hundred strike flights were on tap during the day.

Of course, no strikes in support of the Cambodian ground troops could be put in without the valiant Forward Air Controllers (FACs) who flew their planes low and slow over enemy positions talking to the radio operators of the ground commanders on their FM (Fox Mike) radio. During that period, the Rustic FACs not only played a major role in the Cambodians' fight against the communist Khmer Rouge guerrilla forces, they become close combat partners and friends with the ground commanders and their radio operators. French-speaking Air Force NCOs flew in the backseat to avoid language problems with the French-speaking Cambodians. These young enlisted warriors volunteered from jobs such as clerk typist and airplane fueler and were flying combat within hours of being asked.

Somewhat sub rosa, my office became heavily involved in the prosecution of the air war using these assets. During the time the USAF command post, Blue Chip, powered down at Tan Son Nhut preparatory to reopening at Nakhon Phanom, Thailand, we assumed more control than ever before. We were allowed to import such stalwarts as Maj. Dave Sands and Sgt. Gil Bellefeuille (who had many backseat Rustic missions) who helped us sort out the missions as well as helping set up Cambodian Tactical Air Support Centers. Our main call sign was Area Control and we used personal call signs such as Papa Wolf (Berent) and Dirty Dog (Sands). We became well known on the Cambodian FM frequencies and were often told we were far better than Blue Chip because we made instant decisions. One time we even called on a Rustic OV-10 near Phnom Penh to attack and shoot down a renegade T-28 pilot who just tried to bomb the Cambodian Headquarters and then defect to Norodom Sihanouk in Red China. (The pilot, married to a close relative of Sihanouk, dropped his bombs short and cracked my hooch a bit.)

For Area Control radio communications, I had a Mk-108 radio pallet on my desk with UHF, VHF, FM, and HF radios. I put the generator on the embassy roof. (Later I received more sophisticated equipment.) We dodged the media (except for Denis Cameron and Kate Webb of the UPI, who were on our side) and two congressional aides from Senator Church's office. We also got permission to refuel, but not rearm, the Rustics at Pochentong, the air base and airport outside Phnom Penh. We had a tragedy on the runway when one OV-10 crashed and burned. The black greasy smoke rose over the city as a memorial to a warrior who gave his all for another flag. Two others crashed but survived. We also had a crippled A-7 recover there as well as a badly shot up C-130 whose crew kissed the ground after they hurriedly evacuated the fuel-leaking transport.

Once targets were confirmed by Area Control and the Cambodian DASC (Direct Air Support Center), the FAC would call in a flight of USAF fighters to hammer the communists with a lethal variety of ordnance.

The Rustics were the FACs who logged the most missions and flew the most hours in support of the Cambodian fighting men during those last few months of our war in Southeast Asia.

Hourly, beleaguered radio operators would come up on a Fox Mike radio frequency beseeching air support from the Rustics against the Khmer Rouge. We in the embassy could do nothing, nothing legal, that is. Under the Cooper-Church Amendment we had many restrictions. The primary one was that no American combat troops were allowed on the ground in Cambodia. If fact, the total American presence was limited to a mere two hundred people. And that went from the ambassador right down to a clerk typist in the Military Equipment Delivery Team, Cambodia (MEDTC). We often had to fly out one or two each evening to maintain the level at two hundred.

MEDTC was there because MAAG (Military Assistance and Advisory Group) had become as politically an incorrect word and concept as napalm. A MAAG group was set up in various countries to aid that country's military to become an effective fighting force. Not so in Cambodia. Advising was verboten. Therefore, our MEDTC members (Army, Navy, and Air Force), could only assess what the Cambodian fighting forces needed, could only order the equipment and arrange transportation into Cambodia. They could not legally show them how to put a cartridge into a rifle, much less advise them which way to point the gun. Further, the dollar amount of aid to Cambodia was miniscule compared to that sent to Vietnam.

The Cambodian troops soldiered on. Due to the usual American government ineptitude (typified by a State Department official who refused to forward proof that more than fifty jeeps were given to high-ranking officials rather than to the men in combat), trying to get someone else to do something without controlling the infrastructure even when paying the bills, there was much corruption and incompetence among many of the Cambodian political and military leaders. But the field troops, the ones out on the front line, were doing their job and the Rustics knew this and appreciated their devotion and courage. The Rustics gave the Cambodians just as much courage and skill in return as they have given the American ground troops in Vietnam.

Then, one day, August 15, 1973, a sultry Wednesday, it was all over. One Rustic pilot in an OV-10 trailing smoke did a loop over Phnom Penh. A final salute to a valiant nation. No more American war planes roared through Cambodian skies. All the flight lines in Thailand were silent. Radio calls from besieged ground troops went unanswered. It was over.

Today, if an unknowing individual were to quiz in the wrong manner those Americans who flew combat in Cambodia, they would soon see a black frost in the flyers' eyes. If the questioner were smart, he would press no further or he might find himself on the receiving end of a barrage of anger over the waste caused by cowardly American politicians. Politicians who boldly entered our troops into a war then hamstrung them so much they could not possibly win and hence were forced to abandon allies and friends made in the crucible of war.

Nonetheless, in the Cambodian war the finest of American fighting airmen surfaced and fought the enemy to a standstill. Today, the American people have finally separated the war from the warrior and have come to understand the war was lost on the streets here in the United States, not on the combat fields of Southeast Asia. Exactly as Ho Chi Minh said it would be.

For myself, I could never adjust to the peacetime Air Force when my tour was up. We were all so involved with the Cambodians that we were devastated when the country fell in April 1975. The last word from Sam the Fac, who saved my life more than once, rang in my head. "Too soon to know, too soon to go."

—Mark Berent

Lt. Col. Mark Berent, USAF (Ret.), was first the Assistant Air Attaché then the Air Attaché in the American Embassy in Phnom Penh from July 1971 to August 1973. He had previous combat tours flying F-100s out of Bien Hoa, Vietnam, in 1965–66 and F-4s out of Ubon, Thailand, in 1968–69. He is the author of a five-book Vietnam airwar series starting with *Rolling Thunder.*

Preface

Unlike many stories about the war in Vietnam, this one has a definite beginning and an exact ending. It lasts from June 20, 1970, until August 15, 1973; a little over three years. Also unlike many stories about that war, there was no file of information to use as a starting point. There was no official unit history as the Rustics were never a designated unit. They were a Task Force. The entire operation was managed from the White House and classified Top Secret. The lack of records at that level may have been deliberate. Project CHECO (Contemporary Historical Evaluation of Combat Operations) collected historical data on many aspects of the war. The CHECO report on the American incursion into Cambodia in May and June of 1970 is excellent. Unfortunately, this book starts just after that and there is no CHECO report covering the Cambodian air operation. Contemporary history books cover the politics and ground war in Cambodia, but say very little about the air war.

This book is basically the story of the Rustics themselves and it could not have been written without their contributions. All material quoted or credited to individual rustics or Cambodians is based on taped interviews or on written material submitted by them for use in this book. Other sources consulted are cited in the endnotes for each chapter and referenced in the bibliography.

The title of the book comes from the radio call sign used by the pilots and interpreters flying in Cambodia. They were the Rustics. Almost all of the action takes place in Cambodia, although it is impossible to completely separate those actions from what was going on in Vietnam and Laos at the same time.

The Prologue sets the stage for how it all started and the Epilogue answers some obvious questions about what happened after it ended.

A word about terminology. As Americans, we refer to Cambodia as the country and its military forces as the Cambodian Army, the Cambodian Air Force, and so on. Those were the terms used during the time period covered in this book. To be absolutely accurate, Cambodia, under the Lon Nol regime, was officially the Khmer Republic. Their Air Force was the Armee de l'Air Khmere (AAK) or, more commonly, the Khmer Air Force (KAF). Their Army was the Forces Armees Nationales Khmeres (FANK). The Cambodian opposition was originally termed the Kampuchea Communist Party (KCP), but was called the Khmer Rouge (Red Cambodians) by almost everyone.

For consistency, this book uses the terms in common use at that time.

R.W.

Acknowledgments

For technical review: Doug Aitken, Jim Gabel, Claude Newland, Jim Reese, Dick Roberds; historical research: Jim Gabel, Jim Reese; photo compilation: Doug Aitken; maps: Bill Nelson.

The assistance of Mark Gatlin, the aviation, space, and military history editor of Smithsonian Institution Press, must be acknowledged. His patience, guidance, and advice were invaluable.

This is the story of the Rustics—by the Rustics. These Rustics and their Cambodian friends contributed pictures, written stories, and taped interviews. They responded to questions with e-mails, letters, or phone calls. Without their contributions there would be no story. The are: Tom Adams, Doug Aitken, Bob Andrews, Walt Arellano, Gil Bellefeuille, Mark Berent, Don Brooks, George Brower, Bill Carruthers, Bob Clifford, Don Corrie, Lou Currier, Si Dahle, Ron Dandeneau, Dave Dekoker, Roger Dodd, Don Dorr, Larry Driskill, Jerry Dufresne, Bill Ernst, Walt Friedhofen, Phil Frischmuth, Jim Gabel, Joe Garand, Mick Gibbar, Les Gibson, Don Hagle, Roger Hamann, Bob Harris, Ned Helm, Jim Hetherington, Randy Hetherington, Steve Hopkins, Dave Hull, Hank Keese, Larry Landtroop, George Larson, Bill Lemke, Jim Lester, Nick Lewis, Jerry McClellan, Don Mercer, Marcel Morneau, Clint Murphy, Claude Newland, Jim Nuber, Kohn Om, Lieou Phin Oum, Bill Powers, Jim Reese, Dick Roberds, Jon Safley, Rick Scaling, Don Shinafelt, Jim Siebold, Ray Stratton, Robert (Doc) Thomas, Jim Twaddell, Joe Vaillancourt, Dave Van Dyke, Ron Van Kirk, Bob Virtue, Otto Walinski, Mike Wilson, and Tom Yarborough.

Prologue

In 1970, American pilots in South Vietnam knew exactly where Cambodia was. It bordered three-fourths of South Vietnam and stretched from the Gulf of Thailand northeast nearly to Dak To. On all maps, the border was plainly marked with a heavy red line and its jagged appearance spawned nicknames like the Parrot's Beak, the Fish Hook, and the Dog's Head. The Cambodian side of the border was the terminus of the Ho Chi Minh trail, which originated in North Vietnam and came down like a giant fire hose through Laos and Cambodia. Instead of spewing water, though, it was spewing munitions and supplies to support the North Vietnamese Army and the Viet Cong in South Vietnam.

There were occasional clandestine missions across the border in an attempt to stop this flow of supplies and, in 1969, President Richard Nixon authorized B-52 strikes along the border inside Cambodia. These activities seldom penetrated more than 15 miles (25 kilometers) from the border.

Other pilots treated the border with caution as openly crossing it was a violation of the U.S. Rules of Engagement and could result in serious discipline. That usually meant being grounded pending an investigation. American radar controllers watched the border closely and potential violators were warned on the emergency radio frequency. "Aircraft in the vicinity of ———, you are about to cross the Cambodian border. Turn immediately to heading ——— and identify yourself."

The aircraft would turn, but there was no identification or even acknowledgment. If the radar controller couldn't identify the plane, he couldn't write much of a report.

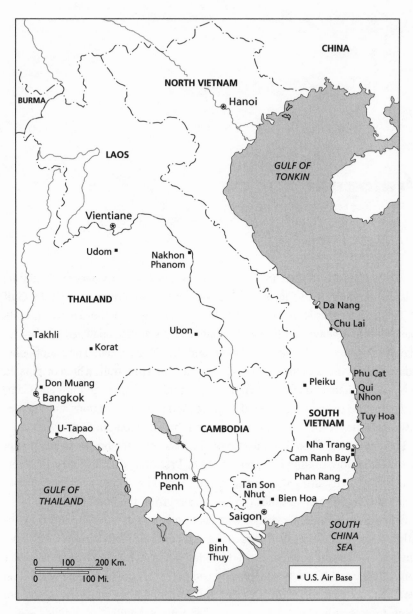

Southeast Asia.

On April 30, 1970, the situation changed. The Army of the Republic of Vietnam (ARVN) and the U.S. Army "invaded" Cambodia with full air support from the U.S. Air Force. The U.S. Army could only stay in Cambodia for two months without congressional approval as that was the maximum time permitted the president under the War Powers Act. The U.S. Air Force, though, continued to operate over Cambodia for the next three years. Because it was highly classified and the directions were coming straight from the White House, there was no official Air Force history of that operation. It never happened.

Here is the story, though, told by the people who were there and did it. It is a story deeply rooted in the politics of the time.

Since 1863 Cambodia had been part of French Indochina and a colony of France. In 1941, the French installed Norodom Sihanouk on the throne of the monarchy believing that he would support the French during World War II. In that war, the Japanese took over most of French Indochina, but allowed the Vichy French[1] to remain in nominal control of Cambodia. In 1945, the Japanese took full control from the French and ordered the royal rulers of Cambodia, Vietnam, and Laos to declare their independence from France. That independence was short-lived, as the French returned after World War II and reclaimed their colonies. In 1953, the French allowed Sihanouk to once again proclaim independence for his country.[2]

Sihanouk's politics were described as a policy of "nonalignment" that was strongly anti-American and pro-Communist. In 1965, he formally broke diplomatic relations with the United States when it sent combat troops to Vietnam in support of the South Vietnamese. In addition, Sihanouk permitted North Vietnam to move supplies down the Cambodian side of the border to South Vietnam. He also allowed supplies to be shipped by sea to Cambodia's only seaport at Sihanoukville (Kompong Som). From there, they were moved by truck to Phnom Penh and eastward to the border with South Vietnam. Some historians estimate that this route carried 80 percent of the supplies reaching the Viet Cong and North Vietnamese troops in South Vietnam.[3]

Meanwhile, a communist party had formed in Cambodia. Initially, this was known as the Kampuchea Communist Party (KCP), but it was soon named the Khmer Rouge (Red Cambodians) by Sihanouk himself. The name stuck and was applied to all Cambodian insurgents opposing the government.[4] For a number of good reasons, Sihanouk felt that his country was facing significant danger from the communists and, in 1967, he offered to reestablish relations with the United States. This did not include permission to put American troops in his country to cut off the flow of supplies and munitions into South Vietnam.[5]

In 1970, Richard M. Nixon was president and "Vietnamization" was in progress. This was a program to get the United States out of the war with a measure of honor and turn all the active fighting over to the South Vietnamese. Americans stationed in Vietnam at that time were involved in a hopeless situation and they knew it.

By 1969, Cambodia's economy was a shambles and political opposition to Sihanouk was growing. Gen. Lon Nol, prime minister and chief of staff of the army, was particularly disaffected. In March 1970, while Sihanouk was on a holiday in France, Lon Nol overthrew the government and took control of the country.[6] Lon Nol was staunchly anticommunist and one of his first acts was to close Cambodia's seaport to communist supply ships and cancel Sihanouk's agreement to allow supplies to be transported down Cambodia's eastern border. He gave the communists seventy-two hours to leave the country.[7]

Lon Nol lacked the military strength to successfully oppose the Khmer Rouge, the Viet Cong, and the North Vietnamese. His entire army consisted of only thirty-five thousand poorly equipped soldiers[8] and his air force had fewer than thirty aircraft with almost no air support capability. He sought American assistance.

On April 30, 1970, assistance came in the form of the previously mentioned invasion as American troops crossed the border to cut the supply lines and eliminate communist sanctuaries in Cambodia. Back in the United States, this was called an "invasion" but it really wasn't. The Americans were there with the full knowledge and approval of Lon Nol.[9]

In the United States, this support of Cambodia was strongly opposed by the Congress, the news media, and much of the public. At Kent State University, four students involved in a demonstration were killed by National Guardsmen. President Nixon could not keep troops in Cambodia beyond the end of June without the approval of Congress—which was not to be had.

The incursion into Cambodia was a tactical success, but it had little lasting value. It destroyed about a year's worth of communist supplies and munitions, but it did not permanently destroy the communist sanctuaries nor did it close down the Ho Chi Minh trail. Both were rapidly rebuilt.

Although President Nixon was forced to remove the troops by the end of June, he did not want to desert the Lon Nol regime, which he now regarded as an ally. He reasoned that he could provide American air support to the Cambodian army as long as there were no American troops on the ground in

Cambodia. He needed a group of forward air controllers (FACs) who could maintain a round-the-clock presence over Cambodia, work with the Cambodians, and provide them with American air support.

That was the birth of the Rustics. Almost overnight a group of pilots, airmen, and airplanes were assembled, assigned the Rustic call sign, and launched on missions deep into Cambodia. Over the three years of their existence, about 250 U.S. Air Force officers and airmen flew as Rustics. This is their story.

1

The Birth of the Rustics

Military flying organizations like to plan missions and practice them while they can still make changes and iron out the bugs. Launching on an unplanned mission builds feelings of anxiety. The support isn't there. They don't have the right people available. Communications are uncertain. They don't know where they are going and there are no maps. There are no clear instructions on what to do when they get there.

That's one big difference between peacetime operations and combat. In combat, you do what has to be done using whatever and whoever is available at the moment. The Rustics started like that.

On June 19, 1970, The U.S. Twenty-fifth Infantry Division had already pulled out of Cambodia. Their USAF FACs, call sign Issue, were based at Cu Chi and Tay Ninh and weren't busy because of the Cambodian pullback. The FAC Air Liaison Officer at Tay Ninh was Maj. Richard Rheinhart. He took a phone call telling him that he and his FACs would be flying deep into Cambodia starting tomorrow. Their call sign would be "Rustic."

The pilots' normal large-scale (1:50,000) topographical maps covered only about 12 miles (20 kilometers) inside the Cambodian border. That was the limit of the incursion into Cambodia. Using small-scale aerial charts, the pilots did some "back of the envelope" (rough) fuel calculations. The OV-10 could make it well into Cambodia, but it couldn't stay very long. It didn't carry that much fuel.

Meanwhile, Lt. Col. Jim Lester, an OV-10 FAC and a staff officer at the Twenty-fifth Infantry Division Headquarters at Cu Chi, also got a phone call.

His was from Col. Perry Dahl, the commander of the III Corps Direct Air Support Center (DASC) at Bien Hoa. The news was that Jim had a new job. He was to position six OV-10s and eight pilots at Tan Son Nhut and report to the Seventh Air Force Tactical Air Control Center for instructions. Jim had himself and Lt. Lou Currier available at Cu Chi. He had Maj. Dick Rheinhart at Tay Ninh along with Capts. Anthony McGarvey and Roger Dodd, and Lt. Dave Van Dyke. He located Capt. Paul Riehl and Lt. Dave Parsons, who were flying out of Song Be under the Rash call sign and supporting the U.S. First Cavalry Division. Those were the original cadre of Rustics and Jim Lester was their first commander. Jim had planned and led the FAC support for the Cambodian incursion and was an excellent choice for the job.

That night, June 19, Capt. Jerry Auth actually flew the first Rustic mission and did it in an O-2. In the early evening of June 19, Seventh Air Force decided they needed a FAC over Cambodia as soon as possible because of the situation at Kompong Thom. They went directly to Maj. Jim Hetherington, commander of the O-2 Sleepytime operation at Bien Hoa Air Base. The Sleepytime FACs flew primarily at night providing air surveillance over the Saigon area and Seventh wanted a highly qualified O-2 FAC to report immediately to Seventh Air Force Tactical Air Control Center for a special mission. Jim's instructor pilot, Capt. Jerry Auth, was already airborne, checking out Capt. Bob Virtue, a newly arrived FAC. Jim contacted Jerry on the radio and told him to land immediately at Tan Son Nhut.

After landing, a staff car took Jerry Auth to Seventh Air Force headquarters while a jeep drove Bob Virtue the 25 miles (42 kilometers) back to Bien Hoa. Jerry's plane was refueled and rearmed while he was briefed on Cambodia and the situation at the Provincial Capital of Kompong Thom. Within an hour he was airborne with a high-ranking Cambodian officer in his right seat.

The flying time for an O-2 from Tan Son Nhut direct to Kompong Thom was well over an hour, which was a long time to navigate in the dark with no lights on the ground, no radio fixes, and nothing but an obsolete map of an unfamiliar country. Night navigation was part of his job, though, and Jerry was very good at it. He flew directly to Kompong Thom and established radio contact with the ground commander. He was well out of radio range of any radio in South Vietnam, but he was in contact with some American gunships. They didn't have the right radios to talk to the ground commander and could do nothing without target identification and positive target clearance. Working with the ground commander, Jerry could identify and mark the targets and he had the Cambodian clearance authority sitting right beside him. Jerry directed

Two O-2A aircraft, minus external stores, fly in formation. Photo courtesy of Richard Roberds.

the fire of the gunships, which reportedly changed the course of the battle that night. A few weeks later, Seventh Air Force recommended Capt. Auth for the Silver Star for that mission.

The next day, June 20, Dick Rheinhart and Dave Van Dyke took off early in the morning from Tay Ninh. Dick flew directly to Tan Son Nhut to fly the first OV-10 mission after being briefed and refueled. There, he also picked up an English-speaking Cambodian officer for his backseat. Dave headed for Bien Hoa to have a long-range (230 gallon) belly fuel tank installed. Lt. Lou Currier, who spoke French, was waiting for him. They were briefed by telephone and launched around noon to replace Dick Rheinhart. Jim Lester and the other four pilots went to Bien Hoa for installation of the 230-gallon fuel tanks and arrived at Tan Son Nhut in mid-afternoon.

Tan Son Nhut Air Base was the main airport at Saigon, the capital of South Vietnam. It was also the headquarters for all American military activity in Southeast Asia. This included Seventh Air Force, which controlled all USAF personnel and aircraft. After parking their planes, Jim and his pilots went directly to the Tactical Air Control Center where they were briefed by its director, Brig. Gen. Walter Galligan.

AC-130 "Spectre" gunship with an infrared sensor and low-light-level TV in the optical dome near the nose. Two 20mm Gatling guns are visible in front of the left main landing gear and the barrels of twin Bofors 40mm guns can be seen behind the landing gear. Ron Van Kirk collection.

According to Jim, General Galligan took out a six-foot strip of teleprinter paper that was plainly marked WHITE HOUSE. TOP SECRET. FOR YOUR EYES ONLY!

He explained that the message contained Jim's orders and his authorization to go into Cambodia and provide American air support to the Cambodian army. Air support could be obtained directly from Blue Chip, which was the radio call sign for the Tactical Air Control Center. Any targets in Cambodia had to be approved by a senior Cambodian official. There were several of them already at Tan Son Nhut and Blue Chip would obtain the necessary approval. Some of the officials might fly on the FAC missions.

The immediate problem in Cambodia was Kompong Thom.[1] It was a provincial capital located about 93 miles (150 kilometers) north of Phnom Penh and it was under siege. The previous night, General Galligan had sent a single O-2 FAC (Capt. Jerry Auth) up there on very short notice and he was able to use some gunships to good effect. Unfortunately, Kompong Thom was well beyond normal radio range and the O-2 didn't have a long-range high-frequency (HF) radio.[2] The OV-10 did have an HF radio and would be able to talk to Blue Chip. The plan was to keep an OV-10 FAC over Kompong Thom twenty-four hours a day and provide whatever air support was necessary to break the siege.

General Galligan told Jim that his call sign would be Rustic and that all the Cambodian army call signs were Hotel followed by a two or three digit number or a word. He gave Jim a list of the known individual Cambodian call signs, their frequencies and the few maps that he had.

The general told Jim to use his outer office for mission planning until he could find him a better place. He reminded Jim that the entire operation was classified Top Secret and the instructions were coming directly from the White House. Very few people knew about the intentions of the United States to provide air support to Lon Nol and the Cambodian Army. The messages from the White House emphasized the need for secrecy.

Dick Rheinhart returned from the first mission and was able to brief Dave Van Dyke on the radio as Dave entered Cambodia to replace him. Capt. Roger Dodd was set up to fly the third mission early that evening. Roger's OV-10 was fitted with the 230-gallon external fuel tank, twenty-eight rockets in four rocket pods, and two thousand rounds of ammunition for his guns. In his backseat, he carried Captain Chiik, a Cambodian Air Force pilot. Captain Chiik didn't have target clearance authority, but he spoke passable English and could interpret conversations with the ground commanders. The OV-10 had a long-range HF radio, so target clearance would not be a problem.

The weather had turned terrible. It was the start of the monsoon season and a torrential rain was coming down. It was so bad that Jim Lester's deputy, Dick Rheinhart, who had returned from the first mission, seriously considered canceling Roger's mission and would have if it had not had such a high priority.

With all the water on the runway and the weight of the extra fuel tank, take-off distance was much longer than Roger expected. Once airborne, he flew on instruments while tracking outbound on a radial of the Tan Son Nhut TACAN. That was a Tactical Air Navigation radio ground station that provided compass bearing and distance information to any aircraft receiving its signal. When the TACAN signal was lost at about 170 nautical miles, Roger kept flying using heading and time until he broke out of the clouds and could see the ground.

Roger got along fine with Captain Chiik, who was a good pilot and had an engaging sense of humor. His night navigation skills were weak, though, and he didn't recognize much of his own country in the dark. They spent a considerable amount of time trying to locate themselves using the outdated maps they had been given. The weather made navigation even more difficult.

They finally made it to Kompong Thom, but without enough fuel to stay very long. Fortunately, it had been a quiet evening at Kompong Thom, probably due to the heavy rains and the work of Jerry Auth, Dick Rheinhart, and Dave Van Dyke. According to Roger, their presence was very welcome and reassuring to the troops on the ground.

The North American Rockwell OV-10 Bronco, built in 1968, was specifically designed for low altitude tactical support. It had two turboprop engines and could carry a variety of stores and ordnance on five stations beneath the belly and on two sponsons. The sponsons were airfoils that drooped down slightly from the bottom of the fuselage. Each sponson contained two M-60 machine guns and could hold one thousand rounds of 7.62mm ammunition for a total of two thousand rounds for all four guns. The standard load for long range missions was a large (230 gallon) fuel tank on the center station and two

North American Rockwell OV-10 Bronco. Doug Aitken collection.

containers of rockets beneath each sponson. Each container held seven 2.75 inch FFARs (folding fin aerial rockets). Of the twenty-eight rockets, half of them had HE (high explosive) warheads while the other half were WP (white phosphorus) marking rockets called Willie Petes.

The tandem cockpit had ejection seats for two crewmen and featured superb visibility along with a total of five air-to-ground radios for communications. It had a large cargo compartment which could carry thirty-two hundred pounds of cargo or five paratroops. Its top speed was slightly over 300 knots (345 mph) and, carrying the 230-gallon fuel tank on the center station, it could stay airborne for nearly six hours.

The plane was fully aerobatic and stressed for eight positive and three negative Gs. It was armored and could absorb a lot of battle damage. It was also quite noisy. The North Vietnamese and Viet Cong called it "the bumblebee" and always knew when one was in the area. Most of the pilots scrounged (and treasured) U.S. Army helmets designed for helicopter pilots. They provided better protection and reduced the cockpit noise level considerably. Its other major defect was a total lack of any air conditioning. Since none of the four canopy hatches could be opened in flight, sitting under the Plexiglas canopy for five hours at low altitude was hot work.

All in all, it was rugged, easy to maintain, and an excellent plane for forward air control work.

Using aircraft to provide control of air support to ground forces was not a new concept. Airborne Forward Air Controllers (FACs) were used to some extent in World War II, but the technique wasn't fully developed until jet fighters were introduced into combat during the Korean War. At low altitude, the jet fighters' fuel consumption nearly doubled and they couldn't stay there very long. At their slowest speed, they were going too fast for the pilots to see any details on the ground. They needed a Forward Air Controller (FAC) who could fly low, slow, and long and could identify the friendly positions and mark enemy locations for the jets. Most of the FAC's work was in direct support of friendly forces and most of the time the friendlies were in direct contact with the enemy. That's when they needed air support and a large part of the FAC's job was to make sure the bombs went on the enemy and not on the friendly positions. In Korea, the North American AT-6 was used as a FAC aircraft. They were called Mosquitoes and the pilots were known as Mosquito pilots.

After the Korean War, President Dwight Eisenhower established a new list of "roles and missions" for the military services. Based on the experiences in Korea, it was agreed that there had to be a FAC present and in control anytime air-delivered ordnance was used anywhere near U.S. ground forces. The Air Force was adamant that a FAC controlling Air Force fighters had to be a fighter pilot himself. The Army argued that it was more important for the FAC to be an Army officer who understood ground warfare. On balance, the Army probably had the stronger argument, but the Air Force won and was committed to providing a fighter-qualified FAC to any Army unit needing close air support.

In Vietnam, the first FAC aircraft used was the Army Cessna L-19 Birddog, which the Air Force acquired and renamed the O-1. In military aviation parlance, L stands for "liaison" and O for "observation." The O-1 served well, but it was limited on the number of radios and marking rockets it could carry. The OV-10 had been ordered, but wouldn't be available until mid-1968, so the Air Force bought some twin-engined Cessna 337 Super Skymasters and designated them O-2As. The O-2A was a significant improvement over the O-1 and it also served well. It is described in detail in Chapter 5.

By 1970, FAC procedures were well established and FACs received formal training at the Air-Ground Operations School at Hurlburt Field in Florida. Rule number one, which came from the "Roles and Missions" doctrine of the armed services, was that if there were friendly forces anywhere in the area, no air-delivered ordnance would be dropped or shot without specific clearance from a FAC. The only exception was for the armed escorts of rescue helicopters. They could shoot at anything. Other than that, the FAC was in charge.

On a FAC mission, the first step was to establish contact with the friendly forces on the ground and learn exactly where they were. Contact was always on FM radio, which was the Army's primary means of communication in the field. All FAC aircraft were FM-equipped, but few other Air Force aircraft had FM radios.

If the friendlies and the enemy were in contact and shooting at each other, it was called a TIC, troops-in-contact. This meant there was active combat in progress and friendly troops needed help. If it was available and there were no weather problems, they almost always received it, and this was when the FAC earned his pay. If the two sides were close enough to shoot at each other, they were also both close enough to feel the effects of any air-delivered munitions. The FAC's job was to make sure that the friendly forces were not injured or killed in the process of attacking the enemy.

Locating the friendly forces was not always easy. In those days before global positioning satellite (GPS) systems, the troops on the ground seldom knew precisely where they were. The FAC had the same maps they had and sometimes the troops could be located by reference to a landmark that both could see. More often it was done by having the ground troops "pop smoke," which meant igniting a smoke grenade. The FAC could see the smoke, even when it had to drift up through the jungle canopy, and establish the friendly positions based on compass direction and distance from the smoke.

Next, the ground troops would identify the location of the enemy by direction and distance from them. The FAC would go to that position and sometimes fire a white phosphorus (Willie Pete) smoke rocket that the friendly troops could see. The friendlies could thus correct the FAC's knowledge of the location of the enemy.

Meanwhile, the FAC had requested air support and sometimes specified the ordnance he wanted. In South Vietnam, he did this through UHF radio to his controlling ground radio station, which used a land line (telephone) to relay the request to Blue Chip. In Cambodia, this didn't work. The FAC was too far from any friendly radio station. Until that problem was solved, the FAC had to use long-range HF radio to talk to Blue Chip. Since only the OV-10 had HF radio and the radio was insecure (it could literally be heard all over the world), this limited operations considerably.

After approving the request, Blue Chip launched fighters or diverted them from some other activity. They were given the FAC's call sign, radio frequency, and a rendezvous point. All Air Force planes used ultra-high frequency (UHF) radios for air-to-ground and air-to-air communication. Blue Chip would select an available frequency and make sure both the FAC and the fighters knew what it was. The rendezvous point was either a plainly recognizable landmark or a radial and distance from a navigation fix. At low altitude in Cambodia, the FAC couldn't receive any navigation signals, but he had marked radials and distances from radio fixes on his map and he knew where they were. The fighters would check in on the frequency and start looking for the FAC. They were at high altitude and had to see the FAC in order to descend and work with him.

Since the FACs had to be identifiable, their aircraft were not camouflaged and the tops of the wings were painted white or light gray. In addition, the OV-10 had a special two-gallon oil tank that allowed a small amount of oil to be dribbled into the engine exhaust. A two-second burst of oil produced a nice white dash in the sky, which made the FAC easy to spot.

The FAC started by telling the fighters what was going on. Since they seldom had FM radios, they really didn't know. They didn't carry topographical maps, so target coordinates meant nothing to them. The FAC described the friendly and enemy positions and told them what their attack direction and pull-off heading would be. He did not allow the fighters to fly directly over the friendlies or even point their ordnance toward them. He told them the target elevation, what he knew of the wind situation on the ground, what they could expect in the way of enemy fire and the location of the nearest safe area in case they were hit and had to eject.

The FAC made sure they had him in sight and rolled in to mark the target with a Willie Pete rocket. The fighters acknowledged seeing the WP smoke and the FAC gave them any necessary corrections. Since the FACs got a lot of rocket practice, the most common instruction was, "Hit my smoke." Next, the FAC switched to FM and asked for final confirmation on target location and told the troops on the ground that the ordnance was on its way. Back on UHF, the lead fighter called "Lead's in, FAC's in sight!" The FAC checked the fighter's position and heading. If they were satisfactory, he said, "Lead, I have you in sight. You're cleared hot." He might also make a small correction to the target. "Put your first bomb 20 meters north of the smoke. Do not drop east of the smoke; that's too close to the friendlies."

Usually the fighters came in flights of two or sometimes three. The FAC cleared them one at a time for as many passes as it took to use all their ordnance or fuel. The code word for being out of ordnance was "Winchester." A plane down to his minimum fuel reserve was "Bingo." Sometimes the FAC would have them hold "high and dry" while he checked with the ground to find out if any adjustments were needed. During all this, the fighters and the FAC watched each other closely for any evidence of ground fire. Enemy fire from assault rifles was hard to spot in the daytime because there was not much of a muzzle flash. Machine gun fire could usually be seen because of the tracer bullets used to help the machine gunner aim his gun. If ground fire was seen, the FAC and the fighters would immediately shift their attention to it.

After the fighters were "Winchester," the FAC would give them whatever BDA (bomb damage assessment) he or the ground commander was aware of. The FAC would thank them on behalf of the ground commander and clear them to return to base (RTB).

The FAC mission was undeniably dangerous. The FAC spent almost the entire flight within range of even small arms fire. Unless the enemy had some sophisticated aiming device, though, the FAC was not an easy target to hit. During rocket passes, he became easier to hit because he was usually lower than normal and the enemy gunner frequently had a good head-on or tail-on shot at him. Normally, though, the experienced enemy soldiers did nothing to attract the attention of the FAC. That would mean instant retaliation, particularly from the OV-10, which carried its own machine guns and HE rockets. Once the FAC started shooting WP rockets, the enemy would usually shoot back. They figured that if the FAC was marking a target, there was a fighter behind him with bombs or napalm and things couldn't get any worse. They might as well shoot at the FAC.

Gunships were used widely throughout Southeast Asia. They were the product of someone's brilliant idea that few thought would work. The original gunship was a modified C-47 called "Puff, the Magic Dragon." Machine guns were mounted in the cabin and fired through holes cut in the left side of the fuselage. The pilot had a rudimentary gunsight rigged near his left shoulder and pointed out his left window. He would put the airplane in a left turn at a planned altitude and airspeed and adjust his bank to line the gunsight up with the target. He could fire all the machine guns with a trigger on his control column. The results were spectacular and someone described it as "a golden hose of bullets sweeping the target." As long as he could identify the target, the pilot could put a stream of concentrated fire on it with remarkable accuracy. He could keep doing it for a long time, because he could carry a large amount of ammunition and fuel.

Once the Air Force learned how effective the gunships were, they began converting transports to gunships and improving their firepower and accuracy. Shadow was the call sign of an AC-119 gunship carrying four 7.62mm mini-gun pods. A later version, Stinger, also carried a 20mm Vulcan cannon. Spectre was an AC-130 that could carry a variety of weapons including mini-guns, 20mm cannon, 40mm cannon, and (in 1972) a 105mm howitzer.

Now that the initial missions were over and a schedule was established, Jim Lester could catch his breath and begin dealing with the organizational problems, of which there were many. Six planes and eight pilots could not maintain the coverage the White House wanted. Few of the Cambodian radio operators spoke English and none of the Rustic pilots spoke Cambodian. Relying on a few English-speaking Cambodians to fly as interpreters was, at best, a temporary solution. There had to be better maps than they presently had and both the pilots and the ground commanders had to be working from the same map. Communicating solely by HF radio was possible, but unsatisfactory. The Rustic pilots were collecting real time information about what was happening in Cambodia, but there was no organized method for dealing with it. The Rustics would need their own dedicated Intelligence section. Finally, flying Top Secret missions from Tan Son Nhut was not going to work. There was no OV-10 maintenance there, no separate living quarters, and no secure operational facilities.

In spite of the problems, the Rustics had started an operation that would last for three years and end only with the cessation of all American operations in Southeast Asia.

2

The Backseaters

The Rustics' biggest problem was language. Few of the Cambodian army units had anyone who spoke English and none of the Rustics spoke Cambodian. Carrying English-speaking Cambodians as interpreters worked, but there weren't enough of them and not all of them understood aviation terminology. Language was still a barrier to communications.

The solution came as the result of Cambodia's heritage as part of French Indochina. Most educated Cambodians spoke French as a second language. All Air Force units in South Vietnam were scoured for French-speaking Americans of any rank to volunteer for a highly classified mission. Pilots were particularly wanted.

French-speakers came trickling in as they were located. The usual procedure consisted of an interview with an officer who wanted them to volunteer for something without giving them any idea what it was. He probably didn't know himself. Those that accepted were interviewed in French by a Cambodian officer to make sure they were actually fluent in French. That was the entire process. There were no application forms, orders, or training schools. The paperwork officially transferring them to the Nineteenth Tactical Air Support Squadron (TASS) would take a while. The next step was issuing them a flying suit, survival vest, parachute harness, .38 caliber revolver, helmet, and a barf bag. That was when they learned they had volunteered to fly combat missions. That was followed by a short briefing on how to climb into the backseat of an OV-10 (a little tricky the first time), how to use the radios and the ejection seat, and what things not to touch. Some of them were flying their first combat mission over Cambodia within a few hours of volunteering. That's how badly they were needed.

For some of them, the barf bag was the most important piece of equipment they carried. The OV-10 was fully aerobatic and could pull as many as eight G's while maneuvering.[1] Air sickness was common until the interpreters became used to the stresses imposed by a high performance aircraft.

Initially, only six volunteers could be found; all enlisted men. Among them were a security police dog-handler, a radio operator, an air traffic controller, a civil engineer, a transportation specialist, and a clerk typist. A mixed group, to be sure, but they shared some common characteristics. They were all volunteers. They were dedicated to their country and the U.S. Air Force. They all fell in love with the Rustic mission and many of them asked to extend their tour of duty in Vietnam. None of them quit.

Sgt. Jerry Dufresne, Rustic India,[2] was a radar operator at the radar control facility in Saigon when the word came down the chain of command to find French-speakers. Jerry's supervisor knew he spoke French and sent him to Seventh Air Force headquarters for an interview. Jerry passed the interview by volunteering for the assignment and demonstrating his French to a Cambodian officer. Next, he met Lieutenant Colonel Lester, the Rustic commander, and was introduced to the pilot he would fly with that evening. Within hours he flew his first OV-10 mission to Kompong Thom.

M. Sgt. Ron Dandeneau, Rustic Foxtrot, was located through the USAF Military Personnel Center (MPC) computer system. The computer knew he was a qualified French linguist because he was tested every three years to maintain his proficiency status. The computer also knew where he was. He was close by in the Traffic Management Office at Tan Son Nhut. He likewise passed the interviews and joined the Rustics. Because of his seniority, he became the noncommissioned officer in charge (NCOIC) of the enlisted interpreters.

"They were all volunteers and that made my job as their supervisor very easy. Colonel Lester was a great commander and made sure that I got everything I needed for my people."

T. Sgt. Joseph R. Vaillancourt, Rustic Hotel, was a communications specialist who was recruited in a Seventh Air Force men's room by a French-speaking USAF colonel. Initially, he was noncommittal, but twenty minutes later another colonel called him and asked him to attend a briefing that afternoon.

After demonstrating his fluency in French and listening to a twenty-minute briefing, he was outfitted with flight gear and introduced to his first Rustic pilot, Maj. Richard Rheinhart, Rustic 02.

"Just call me Dick," he said casually.

Four hours after his recruitment in the men's room, Joe was strapped into his first OV-10. Departure time was 1730 and the target was approximately three hundred North Vietnamese regulars caught out in the open in Cambodia. Dick Rheinhart put in two sets of fighters dropping napalm, and then brought in a Shadow (AC-119) gunship who sprayed the area with his guns. Between the napalm and the tracer bullets, it was a spectacular sight.

Joe also learned what it was like to be shot at. The enemy machine gunners also used tracer bullets and he could see them arcing up toward the airplane.

"I had never been so excited in my life! It was like my first time at the circus when I was a kid. I knew right then that I was hooked on the Rustic mission."

Recruitment took many forms. A1c. Walt Friedhofen and his boss, Sgt. Gil Bellefeuille, were radio operators and roommates at the Third Direct Air Support Center (III DASC) near Bien Hoa. They both spoke French and they were helping establish the Rustic radio relay station on Nui Ba Den mountain (see Chapter 6). They knew the Rustics were looking for French-speakers. Gil was going to spend some time at the relay station and he suggested to Walt that he sign up with the Rustics and find out what was going on. Walt did that and became Rustic Romeo. A month later, he tracked Gil down and got him to join the Rustics, too. Gil was Rustic Tango.

Sgt. Pierre M. Ligondè (Rustic Juliet) was a cook who was recruited right off the Bien Hoa mess hall serving line by another backseater. S. Sgt. George Larson essentially recruited himself. He was a clerk in the Nineteenth TASS orderly room at Bien Hoa when he overheard Ron Dandeneau speaking French with a Cambodian officer. Sgt. Larson introduced himself (in French) and was recruited immediately. He abandoned his typewriter for his new call sign of Rustic Uniform.

Capt. Clint Murphy was the administrative officer of the 504th Tactical Air Support Group (TASG) at Cam Ranh Bay. The 504th was the parent group for all of the FAC squadrons in South Vietnam and Thailand. By August, the Rustics were growing and consuming a lot of 504th TASG resources. Capt. Murphy attended a briefing on their progress, the air war in Cambodia, and their need for French speakers to communicate with the Cambodians. Since he spoke French, he volunteered immediately, but didn't expect to be accepted. He thought there would be more and better qualified people available. He was accepted immediately and was surprised to learn that besides Lt. Lou Currier, he was the only other French-speaking officer in the Rustics. Because of his rank, he became the officer in charge (OIC) of the backseaters. He moved to Bien Hoa and was assigned Rustic Charlie as his call sign.

As the Rustics grew, the need for interpreters also grew. The entire Air Force was searched for French speakers who hadn't yet been to Vietnam and would volunteer for a highly classified assignment. Sgt. Roger J. Hamann (Rustic Yankee) was located at Wurtsmith AFB, Michigan, where he was driving a fuel truck.

> I had taken a French language test in basic training and I had already volunteered to go to Vietnam or Thailand because I was tired of being in the middle of nowhere in Michigan pumping gas into B-52s. Call it ignorance or stupidity, but I just wanted to do something a little more meritorious while serving my country. The next thing I knew, I was going to survival schools, altitude chamber training, and so on, still with no idea as to what I was going to be doing. I never dreamed of actually flying combat missions.

Capt. Hank Keese was an A-37 fighter pilot stationed at Bien Hoa. The Military Personnel Center at Randolph AFB, Texas, discovered that he spoke French and sent him a letter asking if he would volunteer to be a backseater in a secret combat operation in Southeast Asia. Since Hank had already flown combat support missions for the Rustics, he knew exactly what secret operation they were talking about. His A-37 squadron was closing down and he was in danger of being sent to Saigon to complete his tour as a staff officer at Seventh Air Force. Not if he could help it. He knew Lou Currier, knew that Lou's tour would be up in another month, and knew the Rustics had no replacement French-speaking pilot in sight.

Hank flew two A-37 missions in the morning and went over to the Rustic Operations building still wearing his sweaty flying suit. He found Lt. Col. Jim Lester and asked him for a job. He told Jim he spoke French, but didn't want to be a backseater. He wanted the job that would be open when Lou Currier left.

Jim shook his head. "Sorry, but we can't send you to pilot training just because you speak French. It's the backseat or nothing."

Hank looked down at his name patch, the one with pilot's wings on it, to make sure it hadn't come unstitched from his flying suit. "Sir, I'm already a pilot and I just finished flying two A-37 missions in Cambodia for the Rustics this morning."

Jim stared at him, blinked once, stood up, stuck out his hand, and said, "Welcome to the Rustics." Hank was transferred immediately to the Nineteenth TASS and sent to Da Nang for checkout in the OV-10.

Capt. Doug Aitken was also tracked down by the MPC computer. He had been tested for both French and Spanish proficiency in 1965 when he entered the Air Force. In the fall of 1970, MPC found him at Maxwell AFB, Alabama, where he was halfway through Squadron Officer's School. They tried to pull him out of school and send him to Vietnam as a French-speaking pilot, but wouldn't tell him what the assignment was. The lieutenant colonel who was explaining all this to him didn't know either.

"But, sir," Doug said, "I haven't spoken French in five years!"

The colonel didn't crack a smile. "Practice, my son. Practice." Doug negotiated an agreement that allowed him to finish school and go immediately to OV-10 school. He joined the Rustics in May 1971. By that time, Hank Keese's tour was up and Doug became the only French-speaking Rustic pilot for several months.

Eventually, the Air Force realized that the demand for interpreters was going to exceed the supply. They began sending pilots to language school at Monterey, California, to learn French before they were trained as FACs. It was late 1971 before those pilots began showing up.

Because of the initial shortage of French-speakers, the group was augmented by English-speaking Cambodians who were sent, usually four at a time, for thirty days of duty with the Rustics. This helped both the Rustics and the Cambodian Army as their radio operators learned how to talk to the pilots and how air support worked. Most of them were young Army Sgt.s who were inexperienced but well educated. They were absolutely dedicated to their country and their quiet dignity was a contrast to the boisterous behavior of the Americans. When the Rustics moved to Bien Hoa, the Cambodians lived in the same hooch[3] with the Rustic pilots and the French-speaking backseaters. The hooch bar was a lively place with three languages bouncing off the walls.

Many friendships were formed with these Cambodians. When they returned to their units, it was common to hear them use their Rustic call sign when talking to a Rustic FAC overhead. These Cambodians gave the Rustics a good basic understanding of Cambodia, its people, its government, its military, and its enemies.

This original group of backseaters was absolutely essential to the success of the Rustic mission. Without them, there was no mission. Some of them jokingly referred to the pilots as "those really nice guys who drive us to work each day."

Although the backseaters were there primarily to interpret, they all got involved in the mission itself and became part of what were very efficient two-man FAC teams. Normally, the FAC job was a one-man operation and the pilots were trained to do it all themselves. Typically, the OV-10 pilot would strap a small clipboard with frequencies, call signs, codes, and whatever else he needed for that mission to his knee. He would keep track of what was going on by writing notes on the inside of the canopy with a grease pencil. His map bag (containing more than one hundred maps) was tucked to the left of the gunsight on the glare shield above the instrument panel. He kept the binoculars and the camera with the telephoto lens to the right of the gunsight. If he was carrying a tape recorder, that sat on the radio panel to his right and plugged into his helmet. He had five communications radios on board and he could listen to any combination of them. He always listened to at least two of them at once and could select whichever one he wanted to talk on just by turning a wafer switch.[4] He had learned to do that by feel and could tell which radio was talking to him by the way it sounded. Each type of radio had a distinctive background tone and level of clarity.

The OV-10 was a very stable airplane and the FAC could fly it with either hand or no hands at all while he used the binoculars or camera. Even though the pilot could do it all himself, it was a very busy job. Anyone occupying the backseat was not allowed to just sightsee. He was expected to pitch in and help. The French-speakers figured that out immediately and rapidly became part of the team. Some of the backseaters got so good at it that the pilots would give them the map bag, the camera, and the binoculars and count on them to take notes for the intelligence debriefing. Once the backseaters learned how the mission worked, they realized that the pilot didn't need a word-for-word translation. He needed an understanding of what was happening on the ground and where the friendlies and the enemy were. The backseaters learned how to read maps, plot coordinates, and get the information the pilot needed.

Because they could communicate, the backseaters formed a strong bond with the Cambodians. During times when there was nothing going on, the conversation between the backseater and the Cambodian radio operator on the ground turned to homes, wives, children, backgrounds, ambitions, and so on. The pilots missed much of this as they were rarely included in the conversations. Eventually, the backseaters and the Cambodians were able to recognize each other by voice alone and seldom needed call signs.

The backseaters also got free flying lessons. One of the best kept secrets in aviation is how easy an airplane is to fly if the weather is good and the air is smooth. Besides, reasoned the pilot, if I'm wounded, having a backseater who can fly the machine home might be a good idea.

Another unadvertised reason for the flying lessons was that they allowed the pilot to sneak in a short nap on a boring part of the flight. Occasionally, but not often, the whole mission was boring. Walt Friedhofen was flying with a Rustic OV-10 pilot over a huge water convoy on the Mekong River. The Mekong could handle oceangoing vessels as far as Phnom Penh and this was one of the methods used to transport supplies to Cambodia. (This is described in greater detail in Chapter 8.) On this day, they had no radio contact with the convoy and there was nothing going on. The pilot turned the controls over to Walt, who flew up and down the river for about half an hour. Suddenly Walt realized that the pilot hadn't said a word in a while and was probably fast asleep. Walt knew that they burned fuel first from the belly tank so it could be jettisoned if necessary, but he didn't know if the system would automatically switch to the wing tanks when the belly tank was empty.

He decided he better wake up the pilot, which was a matter of shaking the plane hard enough to get his attention. (He probably could have done it by just pulling back on the power. Sleeping pilots are very sensitive to that sound, or lack of it.)

The pilot came alive just in time to switch fuel tanks and went right back to sleep. It was nice to have someone in the backseat who you really trusted.

Some of the backseaters became very good at VR (visual reconnaissance). VR was an important part of the FAC job as it was a primary source of knowledge about enemy activities. It was best done by someone who flew daily over the area and could note small changes to the countryside and the activities of whoever was down there. That pretty well described what FACs and their backseaters did when they weren't actively conducting war. The pilots were trained to do it, but it was all new to the backseaters. They actually obtained some manuals on the subject, set up a training class, and taught themselves VR theory and technique.

During airstrikes, the backseaters had a small advantage over the pilots. As the pilot pulled off the target after a marking pass, the enemy would frequently come out of their hiding places to shoot at the plane as it pulled up. Due to the way the OV-10 canopy was curved, the backseater could see more of this than the pilot could. When he told the pilot what was happening behind them, the pilot could roll the plane inverted and pull the nose through (a maneuver called a "Split S" because it looks like the bottom half of an *S*) and bring his guns to bear on the enemy.

Backseaters also brought with them a set of young eyes. Almost all of them were in their late teens or early twenties. As one of the Rustic pilots, I didn't wear glasses and I could pass the annual vision test, but I was nearly forty years old. One time we were cruising along at about 3,000 feet when my backseater came on interphone.

> "Hey, look! There's an elephant down there!"
> "Where?"
> "Right there. To the left. Just north of that road intersection."
> "You're making this up. I don't see any elephant."
> "No, really. It's there!"

I rolled the plane over and pointed the nose at the road intersection. At about 1,500 feet I finally saw the elephant, a really big one. Suddenly I felt old. That kid back there could see a lot better than I could.

One problem was the matter of recognition of the backseaters. The job of interpreter did not exist anywhere on any Air Force list of specialties and it was not one of the authorized aircrew positions. The pilots, as aircrew members, were all receiving flying pay (technically called "hazardous duty pay") and collecting an Air Medal for each twenty-five combat missions flown. Although the backseaters were told right at the beginning that they weren't eligible for any of that, it seemed unfair, as they were taking exactly the same risks as the pilots. They were flying a steady six days a week, which should have earned them about one Air Medal a month. Jim Lester tried to solve the problem.

"When I was commander, I requested official recognition for the backseaters. I said, 'These guys are flying combat missions every day. They should be getting flying pay and wearing aircrew member wings. I went in with a strong written argument to Seventh Air Force, but nothing happened. They were very valuable to us. They were first-class people who did a great job and fully earned the recognition."

Recognition would eventually come, but it would take a long time. Actually, what they were doing was entirely voluntary. Not only were they not recognized for it, but they couldn't even explain what they were doing to outsiders. Some of them wrote fake letters to their families telling them how dull it was in Vietnam. They could have just quit, turned in their flying gear, and gone back to their previous job.

None of them did that.

3

Cambodia

With a solution in sight for the language problem, the Rustics concentrated on learning their new AO, or area of operations. In the beginning, none of the Rustics knew what was beyond "the fence," as the border was called. Normally, the FAC's AO was small and limited to wherever the unit they were supporting deployed its troops. The FAC was always in radio contact with his base radio station.

In Cambodia, the AO was the entire country, although most of the heavy fighting was to take place in the central region. Except for the OV-10 HF radio, the FAC was out of radio contact with any ground station in Vietnam. He could talk only to Cambodian Army Units and other aircraft. This was eventually solved by construction of a radio relay station on Nui Ba Den mountain and use of high altitude command and control aircraft. (See Chapter 6.)

The Rustics' first maps[1] of Cambodia were out-of-date French maps that had been scaled to 1:50,000 and overprinted with the American grid coordinate system and legends written in English. In addition to the map inaccuracies, the physical appearance of Cambodia changed markedly due to the seasonal flooding that came with the monsoons. Sometimes, there didn't seem to be much relationship between what the pilot could see from his plane and what was printed on the map.

Cambodia is about the size of the state of Missouri[2] and the Rustics covered it all. The southwestern border of Cambodia is the Gulf of Thailand where Cambodia had its only seaport, Kompong Som. Thailand borders the west and

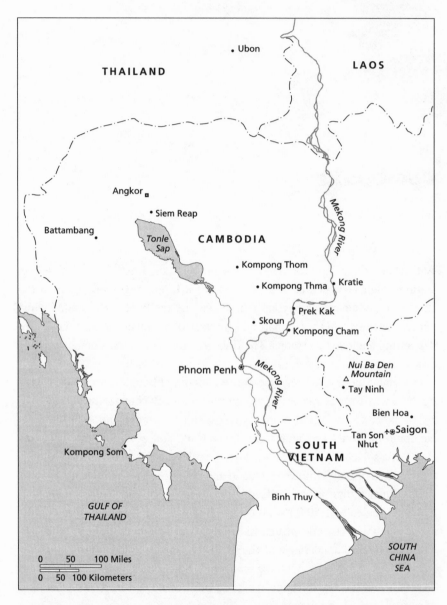

Cambodia, including portions of South Vietnam and Thailand.

northwest while Laos borders the north. The east and south are bordered by South Vietnam.

The two dominating features of Cambodia are the Mekong River and the Tonle Sap. The Mekong is the ninth longest river in the world and larger than any river in the United States. It originates in Tibet and flows south through China, Burma, and Laos to Cambodia. At Phnom Penh, it splits into two branches that both flow to the Mekong delta region in South Vietnam and empty into the South China Sea. The Mekong delta actually extends into Cambodia and the sediment deposited during the wet season flooding contributes to the fertility of the central region. The Mekong is navigable by ocean vessels at least as far as Phnom Penh. During the Sihanouk regime the South Vietnamese considered Cambodia to be an enemy country and did not allow ocean traffic to pass on the Mekong through South Vietnam.

The Tonle Sap, which translates as "Great Lake," is a large lake occupying the west-central portion of the country. It is connected to the Mekong at Phnom Penh by a 62 mile (100 kilometer) river that flows south in the dry season, but reverses and flows north in the wet season. The Tonle Sap spawned numerous small channels and rivers, some navigable by small boats.

Phnom Penh, capital of Cambodia, and the Mekong River. Photo courtesy of Richard Roberds.

The Mekong and the Tonle Sap made aerial navigation reasonably easy, at least in daylight. If the FAC could climb high enough to see either one, he could tell where he was and point the aircraft to where he wanted to go. This form of navigation was called "pilotage," and it went all the way back to the Wright Brothers. It still worked.

Low mountains, with a few peaks rising to 5,000 feet, dominate the southwestern part of the country. The highway from Phnom Penh to Kompong Som passes through the Pich Nil Pass at an altitude of about 3,000 feet.

In the north, there are a few mountains (2,000 feet) near the border with Thailand. South of these mountains are the world-famous temples of Angkor, Cambodia's cultural treasure.

The northeast is mostly plains that become the Eastern Highlands, a remote region of small, but heavily forested mountains and high plateaus. The east, up to the border with Vietnam, is flat and was dominated by rubber plantations.

The central region, where most of Cambodia's population lived, is an area of very fertile and productive farm land. The area produced rice, maize, palm oil, sugar and all varieties of tropical fruit and vegetables. The lakes, rivers,

Angkor Wat, the largest and best known of the temples in the Angkor complex. Doug Aitken collection.

and streams were full of fish and even during bad crop seasons, Cambodia could produce more food than the population could consume. The richest area was a triangle with Kompong Thom at the northern tip, Kompong Cham in the east and Skoun in the west. Although the Rustics ranged over the entire country, this was their primary area of operation.

Cambodia has two monsoon seasons, which strongly influence the Cambodian lifestyle. From November to May, the cool northeastern monsoon blows but brings little rain. This was the dry season. From June to October, the southwestern monsoon brings heavy rains and strong winds. This was the wet season and featured thunderstorms and general flooding of the countryside. The Mekong was swollen and overflowing; the river to the Tonle Sap reversed its course and the Tonle Sap itself increased in size significantly. These seasons affected everything, including military operations. During the dry season, movement was relatively easy. In the wet season, travel was difficult except on the major highways. Small boats replaced the bicycles used in the dry season.

Regardless of the season, Cambodia is hot and humid all year around. Average daily temperatures in Phnom Penh are 85 degrees Fahrenheit (29 degrees Celsius).

Typical Cambodian pagoda. Doug Aitken collection.

From the air, some Cambodian villages looked like they might have been transplanted from the United States. Up to that point, the Rustics' experience with Asian villages came from Vietnam. Most Vietnamese villages looked like someone had dumped a bunch of shacks into a clearing in the jungle. There was no order and nothing resembling streets. The shacks looked like they were all attached to one another and maybe on top of one another.

Cambodian villages, on the other hand, tended to be laid out symmetrically with wide streets and what appeared to be single-family dwellings with lawns and the occasional driveway. Each village had a central market square with a pagoda at one end. The dominant religion of Cambodia was Buddhism, and Cambodian pagodas were elaborate affairs with steeples and colorful spires. Somewhere in each village was a building with an adjoining soccer field that could have been a school.

Cambodia's road system was good for peacetime transportation, but totally inadequate for military operations, particularly during the wet season. It was too easy to block or destroy a road and deny it to vehicle traffic. As an example, Route 4 from the seaport, Kompong Som, was regularly shut down by the Khmer Rouge at the Pich Nil Pass. The Cambodian Army with the help of

Pochentong Airport, Phnom Penh, Cambodia. Doug Aitken collection.

the Rustics could open it, but they couldn't keep it open. Phnom Penh was effectively cut off from its only seaport.

Cambodia had a railroad that connected Kompong Som, Phnom Penh, and Battambang, but none of the Rustics ever saw a train on it. The rumor was that the Khmer Rouge had destroyed all the locomotives.

There were only two airports in the country with hard surface runways. The main one was Pochentong Airport at Phnom Penh, which was both the country's international airport and the primary base for its air force. The other one was at Battambang in the west near the Thailand border. It was used primarily by the Cambodian Air Force for training and was not the scene of intense action as far as the Rustics were concerned. There were some other unpaved airfields at some of the larger cities, but their security was always questionable and they were never used by the Rustics.

Once the Rustics mastered the geography and had visited all corners of the country, they began to develop an appreciation for the Cambodian culture and the beauty of Cambodia itself.

4

Bien Hoa Air Base—July 1970

Operating the Rustic mission from Tan Son Nhut Air Base was never a good idea and it only lasted a few days. There was no maintenance or support for OV-10s and the entire operation was being run out of General Galligan's outer office. The pilots were living in various parts of the officer's quarters and the backseaters were spread out in the enlisted barracks. They were under strict orders to not tell anyone what they were doing and to never speak French in public. That was a little awkward as some of them welcomed the language practice that came from speaking French with each other.

Tan Son Nhut, being the headquarters for the entire U.S. Military Assistance Command in Vietnam, was scheduled to be the last U.S. facility to be closed and it was hopelessly crowded.

On the other hand, Bien Hoa Air Base was only about 25 miles (42 kilometers) north of Tan Son Nhut and had plenty of room. With Vietnamization in full swing, it was already in the process of shutting down. The Ranch Hand operation (C-123s spraying the defoliant Agent Orange) had gone out of business. The Third Tactical Fighter Wing had traded in its F-100s for A-37s and they, in turn, were being gradually turned over to the Vietnamese Air Force. The most active organization on the base was the Nineteenth Tactical Air Support Squadron (TASS).

The Nineteenth TASS was a squadron, but it was actually bigger than most wings. It owned around 150 OV-10s and O-2s plus the pilots to fly them and the mechanics to maintain them. All of the Rustics and their airplanes were technically assigned to the Nineteenth TASS. The reason the TASS didn't look

Bien Hoa Air Base. Picture was taken on a maintenance test flight to check the propeller feathering system. Richard Wood collection.

very big was because they kept the planes and crews at twenty-two different FOLs (forward operating locations) where they were supporting American, Vietnamese, Thai, Korean, and Australian army units. They only kept eight or nine planes at Bien Hoa, which they used for training or as "loaners" for aircraft brought to Bien Hoa for inspection or serious maintenance. The decision to move the Rustics to Bien Hoa was an obvious one and it was done with no break in the mission schedule. The pilots and backseaters merely loaded their belongings into the OV-10 cargo compartment, flew a mission, and landed at Bien Hoa.

In the military, organizations are sometimes thrown together hurriedly to meet a need without much regard for logic. The Rustic organization at Bien Hoa was like that.

In Southeast Asia, the entire U.S. effort was under the command of COMUSMACV, pronounced "Comus-Mac-Vee," which stood for Commander, United States Military Assistance Command, Vietnam. It was commanded by General Westmoreland and later, General Abrams, and was located at Saigon.

U.S. Air Force support was provided by Seventh Air Force located at Tan

Son Nhut Air Base at Saigon. Seventh Air Force was part of Pacific Air Forces (PACAF) headquartered in Hawaii. PACAF, while part of the U.S. Air Force, was under the operational control of CINCPAC (Commander in Chief, Pacific), which was also headquartered in Hawaii. CINCPAC was a joint services command traditionally headed by a Navy admiral. On top of all this, of course, were the president of the United States, the secretary of defense, and the chairman of the Joint Chiefs of Staff.

This organizational structure had existed since the United States entered the conflict in 1965 and by 1970 it was pretty well "set in concrete." Historians point out that one of the United States' major problems in Vietnam was the way the war was managed, or mismanaged, depending on your views. Authority could come from several different directions, but it was hard to establish responsibility.

Into this morass came the Rustics. Their mission orders came directly from the president and bypassed all levels of command between him and COMUS-MACV. In Vietnam, Seventh Air Force owned all FAC assets and managed them through the 504th Tactical Air Support Group at Cam Ranh Bay. The 504th had five Tactical Air Support Squadrons at Bien Hoa, Da Nang, Pleiku, and Binh Thuy in South Vietnam and Nakhon Phanom in Thailand. These squadrons were numbered Nineteen through Twenty-three respectively. Shortly after the formation of the Rustics, the Twenty-first TASS at Pleiku moved to Phan Rang and the Twenty-second TASS at Binh Thuy moved to Bien Hoa. Operational control was from the Seventh Air Force Tactical Air Control Center (TACC) and the Direct Air Support Centers (DASC) in each of the four Corps areas in South Vietnam and at Nakhon Phanom. At first, a Task Force was formed at III DASC under the command of Col. Perry Dahl. This consisted of the Rustic, Sundog, and Tilly FACs. The Sundogs and Tillys both flew O-2s and were established FAC operations in the South Vietnam delta region. They were close enough to begin operating immediately in southern Cambodia. In February 1971, the name of the task force was changed to Nineteenth TASS Task Force, but the operational control remained the same. The Nineteenth TASS was primarily an administrative unit that owned and maintained airplanes and kept track of the people and facilities; but not the mission. That belonged to the task force and their instructions came directly from Seventh TACC. Operationally, the DASCs were bypassed as none of them provided support to Cambodia. At the Nineteenth TASS and task force level, the organization worked quite well. The Nineteenth TASS provided outstanding support and the Rustics took their marching orders directly from Seventh

Some of the original OV-10 Rustics at Bien Hoa, November, 1970. Back row, left to right: Joe Vaillancourt, Doug Hellwig, Don Ellis, Gil Bellefeuille, Paul Riehl, Mike Wilson, Dick Wood, Jim Lester (Commander), Jim Hetherington, Bob Burgoyne, Chuck Manuel. Front row: Don Brooks, George Brower, Clint Murphy, Bob Paradis, Ron Dandeneau, Hank Keese, Greg Freix, Al Metcalf, Jerry Dufresne. Joe Vaillancourt collection.

Air Force TACC. Airborne, they talked directly with "Blue Chip," the Seventh Air Force Command Center.

When the Rustics moved to Ubon, Thailand, in 1971, they became Operating Location 1 (OL-1) of the Twenty-third TASS at Nakhon Phanom. Operationally they were still controlled by Blue Chip in Saigon. That organization also worked well.

When problems occurred, they were usually at the COMUSMACV—Seventh Air Force level at Saigon. Shortly after the move to Bien Hoa, Jim Lester returned to Tan Son Nhut to brief both General Clay, the new commander of Seventh Air Force, and General Abrams, COMUSMACV.

General Clay was briefed first and asked Jim if he had any problems.

> "Yes, we do. I was out yesterday near Kompong Speu and the ground commander said that he had a TIC (troops in contact) about 10 klicks down the road and he needed an airstrike. I flew over there and I could see people running around and shooting, but I couldn't tell the good guys from the bad guys. The only radio they had was back with the commander and they didn't have any smoke grenades to identify themselves. I didn't dare put in an airstrike. If we can't identify the friendlies, we can't help them."
>
> "Did you tell anybody about this?"
>
> "General, I've put this problem in the DISUM several times."
>
> "What's a DISUM?"
>
> "That's your daily intelligence summary."
>
> "Well, who gets that?"
>
> "Your Intell people and your Tactical Air Control Center gets it."

Jim felt like he was talking to a child. General Clay was brand new on the job and he had no idea how the Rustics were organized or how the system worked. Every officer newly assigned to Vietnam went through a period of disbelief at how things were run.

"Well," he said, "we're going over and brief COMUSMACV. We will take care of any of your problems."

Jim and General Clay went into the command center where there were about fifteen generals sitting around a long table with General Abrams at the head. Jim gave him the problem of communications with the ground and identifying friendly forces.

"I thought," General Abrams said, "that we sent them four hundred cases of smoke grenades."

"Yes, sir. We sure did. Those went to Phnom Penh a month ago. I have no idea what happened to them." General Abrams and his staff were right on top of it. They knew exactly what was going on. At the end of it, General Abrams assigned an Army major to move to Bien Hoa and work directly with Jim to resolve those problems when they occurred.

So now Jim had an Army officer on his staff who could make sure the Cambodian Army had the equipment it needed to work with the Rustics. The Army major fit in well with the Rustics, particularly since he brought ten boxes of sirloin steaks with him to Bien Hoa. He obviously understood the supply system.

In the fine print of the daily Top Secret Eyes Only messages from the White House, there was an absolute restriction against landing in Cambodia, anytime, for any purpose. This was strictly political and meant to support President Nixon's claim that there were no American forces on the ground in Cambodia. Nixon felt he could justify the fact that the Rustics were flying over Cambodia, but it would be hard to explain an American combat plane and pilot on the ground. Being on the other side of the world and fighting a war, the Rustics were probably less interested in political happenings in the States than they should have been. This restriction lasted for about a week and was violated about the time the Rustics moved to Bien Hoa.

In late June, Don Shinafelt, an Issue FAC normally stationed at Tay Ninh, returned to Bien Hoa from a week's R&R (rest and recuperation) in Australia. He checked into the Nineteenth TASS and found that all of the Tay Ninh pilots were now flying out of Bien Hoa as Rustics. His personal belongings were on a truck somewhere between Tay Ninh and Bien Hoa. He had only his civilian R&R clothes and one set of flying gear, which he had left with the Nineteenth TASS. The next day, he was flying his first mission as a Rustic. It was an orientation flight for him and he had a Cambodian backseater to show him the territory.

> We were over the Tonle Sap when I heard the Rustic that was supposed to relieve me call and say he couldn't get through the thunderstorms that were lined up along the border. I tried to go back to Bien Hoa, but I couldn't get through them either. The Cambodian in the backseat was urging me to land at Phnom Penh. His family was there and he hadn't seen them for quite a while. I really didn't have much choice.
>
> After landing in the rain and parking the plane, the backseater got us a ride to town and dropped me at a hotel. He was going to pick me up in the morn-

ing. Some Americans in civilian clothes got me some food and a bed for the night. The next morning, we went back out to the airport, fired up the plane and flew it uneventfully to Bien Hoa.

Unless they absolutely had to, the Rustics didn't regularly land at Phnom Penh until 1973, when permission was officially granted to refuel there. As a practical matter, no pilot in his right mind was going to eject and let the plane crash if he could land it safely at Phnom Penh. The Rustics had an open invitation from their Cambodian Air Force friends to land there anytime. When they needed to, they did.

As soon as the Rustics settled in at Bien Hoa, I became Rustic 11 and started flying with them. I had been in Vietnam since mid-March and already had a full-time job as chief of safety for the Nineteenth TASS. I was a fully qualified OV-10 FAC, though, and I could schedule myself to fly a Rustic mission nearly every other day. I also averaged about three OV-10 maintenance test flights each week. They only lasted forty-five minutes or so and were easy to fit into the schedule.

Becoming a Rustic was not a problem. Jim Lester and I had been through OV-10 school together and we were good friends. He needed pilots and was happy to have me, even part time.

The commander of the Nineteenth TASS was Lt. Col. Bill Morton, who had also been with us at OV-10 school. Bill was in his mid-fifties, thin as a rail and topped by a steel gray brush cut. He hadn't flown actively for several years, but he loved the OV-10 and was a very good pilot. He few several Rustic missions as Rustic 10.

Bill once told me that he had the distinction of being the senior ranking lieutenant colonel in the entire U.S. Air Force. He had been passed over five or six times for promotion to full colonel, a situation that would encourage most people to retire. Bill loved what he was doing, though, and intended to hang around for as long as the Air Force would let him.

Being passed over for colonel was no disgrace as the promotion opportunity for that rank was something less than 20 percent. A lot of really good officers didn't make it, Bill Morton among them. Based on its size, the Nineteenth TASS should have had a full colonel for a commander. They were lucky to have Bill.

That camaraderie among us was very helpful. The Nineteenth TASS maintained the Rustic planes and took care of all the personnel matters involving the pilots and backseaters. Bill made sure of that support and Jim was free to concentrate strictly on the mission. Occasionally, the Rustics would lose a mission due to weather, but since the TASS had spare aircraft, they would never lose one to maintenance or aircraft availability. As a maintenance test pilot, I kept the spares ready and became the primary recoverer of aircraft landed at Phnom Penh. The OV-10 cargo compartment could carry tools, parts, or an engine for either the OV-10 or the O-2 and the backseat could carry a mechanic. I made the Phnom Penh recovery trip about six times.

The move to Bien Hoa did not make everyone happy. Like the camel sticking its nose into the Arab's tent, the Nineteenth TASS and the Rustics were beginning to take over Bien Hoa. Within a few weeks, the TASS had moved into a vacated Third TFW (Tactical Fighter Wing) squadron building, many of their maintenance hangars and an aircraft parking ramp in prime real estate. The Rustics moved their pilots and backseaters into a vacant fighter squadron hooch (complete with bar) and took over part of the Third TFW Operations building for their intelligence section.

The base commander (who was also the commander of the Third TFW) did not like the Nineteenth TASS, the FACs, or their airplanes. In retrospect, his

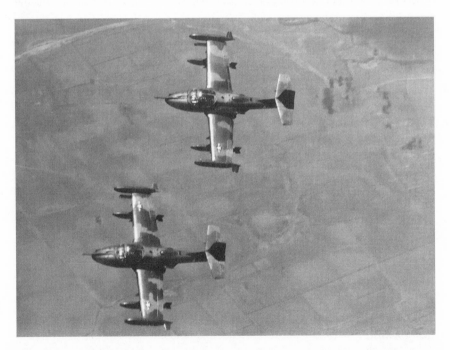

Two A-37s from Bien Hoa. These were the Rustics' favorite fighters for close air support. Doug Aitken collection.

dislike was somewhat understandable. The Nineteenth TASS did not look or act like a real Air Force organization. Most of the FACs and mechanics were based at army forward operating locations and were living the same way the army grunts lived. There were no barbers out there and shaving was optional. The FACs learned that the official Air Force flying suits did not hold up well in the field. They usually wore whatever the army was wearing, which varied from camouflaged fatigues to Australian shorts and bush hats. Flying long missions at low altitude in a hot humid climate was a hot, smelly business and laundry services were not always available. The FACs based with the First Cavalry Division at Quan Loi were recognizable at several feet because their clothes all had a peculiar reddish tinge. Quan Loi had a unique red mud that attached itself to everything and would not completely wash out.

The planes were even worse. Few of the FOLs had paved runways. The FACs were operating from dirt strips occasionally smoothed with the army's tar-like version of instant asphalt. That stuff stuck to the planes like Quan Loi mud. Since water had to be trucked in, nobody wasted it on washing the airplanes.

In addition to being dirty, planes based at FOLs tended to pick up unusual paint jobs and nose artwork, usually in the colors of the army unit. The fuselage frequently acquired a large decal reflecting the unit's coat of arms. The Air Force had its own paint scheme for its airplanes and any variations or additions were strictly prohibited. Those planes had to be kept hidden from Air Force inspectors. The FACs always disclaimed responsibility for this and swore that the army grunts (who loved the FACs for their air support) would sneak up on a plane at night and give it a free paint job. They did the same thing to their own helicopters and, to them, it was a matter of pride. As far as the grunts were concerned, those FACs and airplanes were theirs. This suited the FACs, because after a few weeks at an FOL, they tended to identify more with the Army than the Air Force.

On any given day, the Nineteenth TASS probably had four or five FACs and their airplanes visiting from one of its twenty-two FOLs. The planes were brought in for major maintenance or inspection and the FACs were there on a shopping trip to pick up anything needed by anyone back at the FOL. The visiting FACs would stay overnight and always treat themselves to a few drinks and a steak dinner at the Bien Hoa Officers Club—wearing whatever they flew in with.

This constant presence of dirty airplanes with illegal paint jobs and ratty-looking pilots was probably responsible for the wing commander's anti-FAC attitude. In addition, he was losing authority, real estate, and facilities to the Rustics and the Nineteenth TASS. His job (as he saw it) was to close the base down and give it back to the Vietnamese. Here he had this outfit that was growing like a weed and looking seriously at taking over his personal office, quarters, and staff car. What really annoyed him was that whatever the Rustics were doing, it was Top Secret and he wasn't allowed to know.

The last straw came when he found out that the Rustic pilots and their enlisted backseaters were all living in the same hooch and drinking at the same bar. Officers and enlisted men living in the same building? Absolutely not! Since he was a full colonel and neither the Rustics nor the Nineteenth TASS had one of those, the confrontations with Jim Lester and Bill Morton got a bit heated. About two weeks after the Rustics arrived, he ordered Jim Lester to move the enlisted people out of the Rustic hooch and put them in the enlisted barracks. That would defeat the Top Secret security Jim was trying to maintain among the Rustics, but the wing commander wasn't buying that argument.

> "I said, 'Yes, sir.' Then I called General Galligan at Seventh Air Force and said, 'I'm having to move my enlisted people out of the Rustic hooch.' He asked me why I was doing that. I told him I was ordered to do it.
> " 'Who ordered you?'
> " 'The Wing Commander.'
> " 'That son of a bitch. That's none of his business. Don't move them out. I'll talk to him.' "

Meanwhile, the wing commander went to Col. Perry Dahl, Jim's immediate superior and told him to get rid of Jim. He didn't want him on his base.

"I told Perry that he might as well do that and get someone to replace me who either outranked him or could get along with him. Perry told me to quit worrying. He'd take care of it."

A week later, the wing commander was reassigned as an assistant to General Galligan at Tan Son Nhut. Two weeks later, armed with a new security clearance, he was back at Bien Hoa to be briefed on the Rustic operation. Afterward he told Jim Lester what a great job the Rustics were doing and went back to Tan Son Nhut. Jim already knew they were doing a great job. He also knew that the Rustics were emerging as the most active military operation in the entire theater. They would get whatever support they needed.

Throughout the late summer and fall of 1970, the Rustic operation continued to grow. At Tan Son Nhut, there had been only eight FACs, six aircraft, and a handful of backseaters. In four months, the operation had grown to fifty-two aircraft, seventy FACs, twenty interpreters, ten radio operators, and ten intelligence specialists. Considering that the Nineteenth TASS was handling all the logistics and maintenance and still operating FAC detachments at several FOLs, the total operation was one of the largest USAF operations in the war.

Initially, FACs came from other III Corps locations to become Rustics and the Nineteenth TASS juggled its aircraft resources to support them. This worked for a couple of months, but eventually the Nineteenth TASS's parent group (504th Tactical Air Support Group at Cam Ranh Bay Air Base) began sending in FACs and aircraft from all over South Vietnam and Thailand. The Rustics had top priority on resources and growth sometimes happened over night. At one time, the Seventh Air Force Director of the Tactical Air Control Center told Jim that he wanted another FAC available over Cambodia twenty-four hours a day in addition to the ones they already had.

> I told him that would take another six airplanes and at least eight more pilots. He picked up the phone and called a two-star general—I don't know who—and told him to move six planes and crews to the Rustic operation at Bien Hoa. I could tell from the conversation that the two-star didn't like that at all. The director told him that he didn't care whether he liked it or not. He could either do it or meet him upstairs to discuss it with the four-star. The planes and crews arrived the next day.

One of the first things Jim Lester did at Bien Hoa was to set up a FAC training school for Cambodian radio operators and pilots. Cambodia would send in small groups of Cambodians to spend a few weeks with the Rustics and learn something about the FAC business. Claude Newland (Rustic 19) organized some of the early training courses. Since few of the students spoke English, the course was taught mostly in French by the backseaters.

One of the students in the first class in September 1970, was one of Cambodia's most experienced fighter pilots, Capt. Kohn Om.[1] In the late 1950s, Om was sent to France to be trained as a pilot by the French Air Force. There, he learned English out of a book, *Fundamentals of American English,* which he carried with him at all times. Back in Cambodia in 1964, he was taught to fly the Russian MiG 15 and MiG 17 by an instructor who spoke only Russian. At the Rustic FAC school at Bien Hoa, Om flew as a backseater in the OV-10 almost every day and got to know most of the pilots. As part of the course, the Rustics provided handout material translated into French on radio procedures,

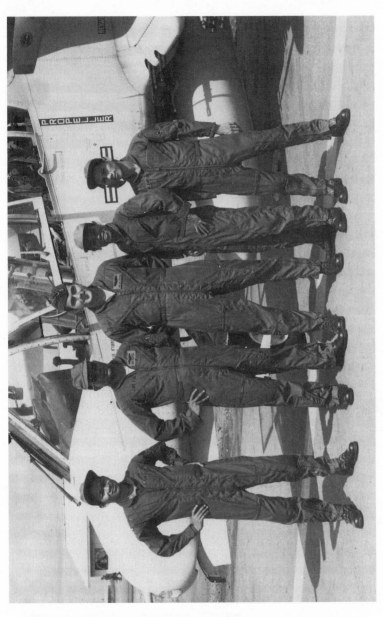

Claude Neland (Rustic 19) with four Cambodian officers he trained at the Rustic FAC school at Bien Hoa, October 1970. Left to right: Lieutenant Huot, Captain Kohn Oum, Captain Ouem, Lieutenant Sophan. Kohn Om was an experienced Cambodian Air Force fighter pilot who worked with the Rustics throughout their existence. Note OV-10 in the background with belly fuel tank, sponson machine guns, and rocket pod. Claude G. Newland collection.

rules of engagement, weapon selection, and a host of other subjects. Kohn Om took all of this material back to Cambodia and set up a FAC school there for young NCOs.

Om had a standing invitation to return to Bien Hoa when he could and lecture to any FAC class that was in session there. When Om was flying a Cambodian fighter, he would always tune the Rustic frequency to talk to the pilots and backseaters he knew and find out if they had any targets for him.

During their early flights in the central region of Cambodia, the Rustics met another Cambodian officer. They were regularly in contact with Hotel 303. This was Col. Lieou Phin Oum, then a major. In the next six months he would be promoted twice and, to avoid confusion, he will be referred to as Colonel Oum.

Colonel Oum turned out to be Cambodia's best military leader. Oum was originally trained in both the United States and Cambodia as an Air Force communications specialist. He later attended senior military schools and became one of the Cambodian Army's most dependable commanders. He was very well educated and his command of English was almost perfect. Regardless of the situation, he was unfailingly courteous and polite and all the Rustics became familiar with his somewhat clipped and formal manner of speech.

"Rustic [his pronunciation was closer to *Roostic*] this-is-Hotel-Tree-Oh-Tree-how-are-you-today-sur?" During radio conversations, Oum would provide the Rustics with current estimates of enemy strength, location, and plans. These were invariably accurate. For several months, the Rustics knew him only as a voice on the radio and didn't realize he was a senior officer until he visited the Rustics at Bien Hoa.

Life at Bien Hoa was not bad. It had most of the conveniences of any large Air Force base including a base exchange, post office, library, chapel, swimming pool (left over from the French) officers club, enlisted club, and mess hall. The toilets flushed, the showers worked, the officers' hooches were air-conditioned, and the hooch maids took care of the laundry. After a sweaty day of flying, it was nice to come home to an air conditioned room, a shower, clean clothes, and a beer. Most of the FACs weren't used to such luxury, but they rapidly adjusted. They started wearing official USAF flying suits and looking like real Air Force pilots. The Nineteenth TASS kept their airplanes clean and painted the way they were supposed to be painted.

Among the drawbacks were the regular rocket attacks on Bien Hoa. These were Russian-made 122mm rockets that packed about 30 pounds of high explosives. They stood a little over six feet tall and were about eight inches in diameter. The rockets were all transported down the Ho Chi Minh trail and hand-carried to launch positions near Bien Hoa.

The typical rocket attack occurred in the wee hours of the morning about twice a week. It consisted of five to ten rockets fired very rapidly. The entire attack seldom lasted more than a minute or two, although it seemed longer.

It was always assumed that the targets were the fuel storage tanks, the bomb dump, or the aircraft, and that the mess halls and hooches were relatively secure. Unfortunately, the aiming and launching methods were very primitive and the rockets might hit anything. Nothing was safe. Americans learned to appreciate what the British must have felt during the V-2 rocket bombardment of London in World War II.

Each building had an area reinforced and sandbagged and designated as the rocket shelter. If you were suddenly aroused from a sound sleep by the explosion of a rocket (followed by the rocket attack warning siren; the normal sequence) and you knew the attack wasn't going to last very long, running for the shelter didn't make much sense. Most just grabbed their flak jacket and helmet and rolled under the bed. The buildings were all sandbagged to a few feet above floor level so this offered some protection from anything but a direct hit.

One of the daily pleasantries enjoyed by the Rustics at Bien Hoa was the company of their mascot, "Missue." Missue was a small, cute, intelligent, and well-behaved dog of uncertain breed. She was originally acquired by the Issue FACs at Tay Ninh and was brought by truck to Bien Hoa when the Issue FACs became Rustics. Her name was a contraction of "Miss Issue." She lived in the Rustic hooch and had the full run of that building and the Operations building. Jim Gabel, the Rustic Intelligence Officer, was particularly fond of Missue.

One of the worst things that happened in 1970 during our Christmas "vacation" was the disappearance of Missue. I was probably the last one to see her on New Year's Eve. As I was coming home from work about 2100, I met her going toward the Ops building. It didn't take much coaxing to get her to follow me back to my room, where I treated her to a jar of dried beef. It was my birthday and I figured someone should help me celebrate.

After she disappeared, we all felt that as plump and well-fed as she was, she probably ended up downtown as someone's New Year meal. Nineteen-seventy had been the year of the dog, so she was reasonably safe. With the dawn of 1971, though, her immunity was gone.[2]

By January 5, I had given up hope of seeing her again. We had another dog named Candy, but she just couldn't replace Missue with any of us.

Then on January 10, Missue reappeared. She just walked up to the door of

"Missue." The OV-10 Rustics' mascot. Doug Aitken collection.

the Ops building, apparently very happy to be back. She was much thinner and smelled like she had spent the entire time in a sewer. After cruising the building and saying hello to everyone, she settled down on her usual place on the floor of the briefing room. The sewer smell was more than I could stand so I took her to the hooch where I washed her in the shower with some Prell shampoo. She wasn't too happy about that, but perked up when I fed her the steak I had thawed for her.

The message, "Missue's back," went out by radio to the Rustics already flying that day and was passed to our Cambodian friends who had been to Bien Hoa, knew her, and knew she was missing. It is amazing how much love can be lavished on a dumb animal. She was a surrogate for all the wives, girlfriends, and families left back home.

At Bien Hoa, the Rustics acquired an extra backseater. Maj. Robert (Doc) Thomas was a flight surgeon at the Bien Hoa medical facility. Although he was assigned as a doctor, he spent as much time as possible with the various units on the base, particularly the Rustics. The two French-speaking Rustic pilots, Lou Currier and Hank Keese, frequently had an empty backseat that Doc

Thomas could fill. The Rustics figured that having their own doctor available was a pretty good idea, so they gave him his own call sign, Rustic X-Ray. That seemed appropriate. As a result of his flights with the Rustics, Doc Thomas became the local arms and munitions merchant.

It all started as the result of one mission with Hank Keese. I think we were flying over Kompong Chhnang, but I was always lost. We saw a well-armed guerrilla unit chasing Cambodian Army soldiers who appeared to have only a few Enfield carbines, probably of World War I vintage. Our government was not supplying Cambodia with arms, and they obviously needed help.

That night, I was at the First Cav. [U.S. Army First Cavalry] area where I saw them getting ready to destroy a pile of captured enemy weapons. I told them that we had some allies who were fighting without any reliable weapons, and that it would be a real payback to the Viet Cong if their weapons were sent back into the field to be used against them and the NVA. The Cav liked that idea and pretty soon the word spread all the way to their headquarters at An Loc.

I started getting jeeploads of weapons, which I stored in my room. My roommate moved out. It became a joke in the Rash hooch where I lived that if we were hit by a rocket, the secondaries would go off for a week. I'm not sure they were joking. The Navy SEAL team, who usually drank with us, brought in their captured RPGs (rocket-propelled grenades), and the Green Beret outfit contributed some captured explosives.

It just kept piling up and I wasn't sure what to do with it. Then we got word that an Air Force inspection team was coming and we had to do something. Through the Rustics, we got word to Col. Oum and he arranged for a Cambodian C-47 to land at Bien Hoa and pick up the pallets of arms and munitions. That was pretty hectic and probably illegal, but every now and then we did something right.

Actually, there was another small source of arms for the Cambodians. Bien Hoa was one of the major aerial ports of entry and exit; the others being Da Nang, Cam Ranh Bay, and Tan Son Nhut. Each day, "Freedom Birds" (commercially chartered transports) would arrive daily to take U.S. personnel of all services back to the United States. Preboarding procedures included exchanging all the military scrip (called Mickey Mouse money) for dollars and a thorough inspection for arms and ammunition being taken home as souvenirs. Since no one wanted to be pulled off the flight to explain why he had an AK-47 in his luggage, the passengers tended to "donate" the weapons before they were discovered and taken from them.

Since the Rustic Intell shop had become the senior intelligence organization on the base, all of these weapons were turned over to them for "examination and proper disposal." To the Rustics, this meant shipping them to Cambodia. The Cambodians attending the Rustic FAC school were delighted to handle the transportation details. The souvenir take from seven flights per week and three hundred passengers per flight could be quite substantial.

Just as the FACs had identified with the U.S. Army units they were supporting, they now identified with the Cambodians.

5

The Night Rustics

Within a few days the Rustics were maintaining twenty-four-hour coverage over Cambodia and running short of airplanes. Jim Lester went to his boss, Col. Perry Dahl, and told him he needed more airplanes and pilots. Jim suggested that the night missions could be given to the Sleepytime FACs who flew O-2s from Bien Hoa. Jerry Auth, a Sleepytime FAC, actually flew the first Rustic mission on June 19. A couple of other Sleepytime FACs had "filled in" on Rustic night visual reconnaissance missions. By virtue of their common training, FACs could switch missions without difficulty.

"They had about eighteen O-2s flying night rocket cover to protect Saigon. They did almost all their flying at night and were using the night vision starlight scopes which we couldn't use in the OV-10. They were all qualified FACs and they could be trained on the Rustic mission."

Colonel Dahl agreed and the Sleepytime commander, Maj. Jim Hetherington and his pilots became Rustics. They still flew the Sleepytime mission, but the need for that was dropping off. The Sleepytime FACs were already based at Bien Hoa and the Rustics were in the process of moving there, so that wasn't a problem. Their primary mission was providing continuous nighttime combat air patrol (CAP) for the Saigon/Tan Son Nhut Air Base complex.[1] That mission was never popular among the O-2 pilots. Most of the time, it was a monotonous three and a half hour flight "boring holes" over Saigon with no action. As Vietnamization increased, the Sleepytime sorties dropped until, in the spring of 1971, they disappeared altogether.

Jim Lester, Rustic Commander, with some of the original O-2 night Rustics, November 1970. Standing left to right: Jim Lester, Mick Gibbar, Don Hagle, Drake Green, Don Mercer, Jim Hetherington, Bob Messer. Front row: John Litton, Dave DeKoker, Bill Lemke, Tom Canter, Wayne Baker. George Larson collection.

The O-2 was the Air Force version of the Cessna 337 Super Skymaster. Except for greater fuel capacity, munitions capability, more radios, and additional windows on the right side, there was little difference between the O-2 and the Cessna 337. The airplane had twin tail booms and two centerline-mounted engines (one forward and one rear), which gave it twin engine performance with single engine handling qualities.

There were two versions of the O-2. The O-2A, the FAC version, had two pylons under each wing for munitions and added windows in the right door and lower right front fuselage to improve pilot visibility. The O-2B was built for psychological warfare. It had loudspeakers and a leaflet drop system, but no munitions pylons.

The O-2 had a top speed of 192 knots (221 mph) and a range of a little less than 1,000 miles. Its design gross weight was 4,300 pounds, but the Air Force consistently operated it at 4,800 pounds or more.

The O-2 had one advantage over the OV-10. Its windows could be opened in flight and a night vision starlight scope could be held out the right window.

An AR-15 assault rifle could also be fired out the right window. This was strictly forbidden because of the risk of hitting the aircraft, but it did happen occasionally. The OV-10's canopy could not be opened in flight and its curvature produced a reflection of the cockpit instrument lights which made the OV-10 difficult to use in night combat missions.

As soon as the Rustic OV-10s were settled at Bien Hoa, Jim Hetherington became Jim Lester's deputy and picked up the call sign Rustic 02. He took over scheduling of the Rustic flying operation, both O-2s and OV-10s. In size, both the OV-10 and the O-2 operations were growing and it soon became obvious that each needed its own commander and Jim Lester needed to be able to devote his time to issues affecting the whole task force. Since Jim Hetherington had originally been trained as an OV-10 pilot, he regained his currency in the aircraft and took over as commander of the day Rustics. Maj. Richard M. Roberds arrived and replaced him as commander of the night Rustics, a position he held until the O-2 Rustic mission was discontinued in September 1971. By January 1971, Jim Hetherington and Dick Roberds each had about thirty-five pilots under their command.

Because it did not have the OV-10 cockpit glare problem and could use the starlight night vision scope, the O-2 was a better aircraft for night missions. Backseaters (interpreters) would fly O-2 missions occasionally, but there weren't enough of them to put an interpreter on every flight. Because of this, it was arranged that English-speaking Cambodian commanders and radio operators would be available at night to talk to the night Rustics. Also, the O-2 pilots had three fluent French-speakers, Lt. Mick Gibbar (Rustic 25), Lt. Wen Pells (Rustic 50), and Lt. Don Mercer (Rustic 41). A few others knew enough French to get by in a pinch, so language was seldom a serious problem.

The standard nighttime O-2 crew was two pilots in the front seats. Just staying visually oriented and navigating in the dark with no lights on the ground and no radio fixes was a two-pilot job. Generally, the right-seat pilot handled the communications with the ground, the starlight night vision scope, and the identification of targets. The left-seat pilot flew the plane, controlled the fighters and marked the targets.

The four wing pylons on the O-2 were numbered one through four starting with the outboard pylon on the pilot's left. The standard Rustic O-2 munitions load was four parachute flares on the number one pylon; two parachute flares on number two, a "log marker" on number three, and a LAU-59 rocket pod with seven WP marking rockets on number four pylon.

The log marker, which looked like a log but was officially called a target

A night Rustic salvos his rockets. The Mekong River is in the background. Photo by Bill Carruthers, Jr.

marker, was dropped by parachute and would ignite on impact and burn with a brilliant red flame. This was visible for 10 miles (17 kilometers) and provided an excellent reference point for the FAC and the fighters. The parachute flares would ignite as they descended and provide 2 million candlepower of light for about three minutes. This was called "lighting up the world," and it allowed the fighters to see both the target and the FAC.

Conducting air strikes at night required a lot of teamwork between the Rustic pilots and the fighters. The left-seat pilot would specify an orbit pattern and a run-in heading for the fighters. He would set up a holding pattern on the side opposite the fighters' pattern where he could see both the target and the fighters continuously. He would, considering the wind, drop a flare where it would provide illumination, but not be blown away from the target or into the fighters' pattern. He would mark the target with a WP rocket and adjust his pattern to drop the next flare as the first one burned out. When the fighters had positively identified the target and the smoke marker, he would clear them "hot" to drop their munitions. This type of teamwork was almost an art form.

All aircraft operating at night in Cambodia flew "blacked out." This was excellent protection against being shot down, but it raised the midair collision potential considerably. Everyone in the air tried to keep track of everyone else in the area and maintain altitude separation.

One dark night David "Zeke" DeKoker was flying with Mick Gibbar in his right seat. They were working with Hotel 21, whose radio operator was Lt. San Sok, who preferred to be called Sam. He asked for an air strike on an enemy storage area and troop concentration he had identified. Zeke ordered fighters through Rustic Alpha, the relay station on Nui Ba Den mountain. Shortly, two A-37 fighters, call sign Hawk, checked in on UHF. While Mick was talking to Hotel 21, Zeke briefed the fighters to set up a 4,000 foot right-hand orbit with a run-in heading of 180 degrees. Zeke was at 2,500 feet. He "lit up the world" with a flare and marked the target with a smoke rocket. The fighters confirmed the mark and were cleared hot, lights off.

As the second fighter pulled off, Zeke saw a concentrated stream of tracers from an automatic weapon on the ground arcing up toward the fighter. Zeke marked the gun position with a rocket and cleared both fighters in hot.

Zeke was maneuvering to drop another flare when Mick suddenly yelled, "Look out, Zeke, he's coming right at us!"

"I looked quickly to the right and all I could see was the belly of an A-37 filling our windshield. Instinctively, I pushed the plane left and down to avoid the collision. We probably missed by less than ten feet."

The fighters had departed from their assigned run-in heading, which put the second fighter on a collision course with the O-2. Since everyone was flying with no lights, there was no way to see another aircraft unless it was illuminated by the light of the flare.

As it turned out, the air strike was a success. The gun was silenced and there were several secondary explosions during and following the strike. Thanks to some luck and the coordination of the two pilots, they were still alive to talk about it.

The ground radio operator, Lt. San Sok (Sam) was an interesting person. All the Rustics worked with him at one time or another and he exemplified the gracious nature and indomitable spirit of the Cambodian people. Sam was a history teacher who spoke excellent English as well as several other languages. He had joined Lon Nol's army to resist the communist aggression in his country. During occasional lulls in the war, a conversation with Sam became a lesson in history and culture taught by an articulate and courteous teacher.

Bob Harris, Rustic 33, first talked to Sam on a night flight in late March 1971. Bob had acquired the nickname "Redeye" as a result of being elbowed in the eye during a pickup basketball game at the Rustic O-2 hooch. This gave him a real shiner, which included a dark red eye socket and a red eyeball that seemed to last forever. Somehow, Sam knew this. Bob contacted Sam and taped the following conversation.[2]

> "Roger, Rustic Redeye, this is Hotel Sam. You know all Rustics and Shadow that is our friends. We have received a debt, but we never repay them. We are very sorry that we couldn't repay them."
>
> "Roger, Sam, I understand, but we are very proud to do it and don't worry about paying us back. We are very proud to do it."
>
> "Understand, sir. Understand you very much. But, anyway, Sam is still on your side, during whole of his life, anyway and anywhere and at anytime. He is always on your side."

All Rustics who talked with Sam were impressed with his commitment, sincere appreciation for their help, and concern for their safety. This concern always amused the Rustics. In their view, Sam's job was much more dangerous. The Cambodian culture, though, always put concern for others first.

Dave "Zeke" DeKoker worked with Sam again on what he called a textbook mission. It was a dark night and Sam requested air strikes on what his troops had reported as a Maj. enemy troop concentration. The target coordinates were only a couple of kilometers north of his position along Route 6.

"Many VC," Sam said. "You come bomb, Rustic Zeke, you come bomb. OK?" While waiting for the fighters, Zeke put out a flare and checked the target with binoculars. It was a large, low, flat building and the map said it was a school. Zeke checked this with the ground commander, Hotel 21, and he emphatically answered that the school was exactly what he wanted destroyed. He said there were "many, many enemy hiding in there," and there were no children or civilians in the school. They had all withdrawn to his position several days earlier.

Hotel 21 had always been right in the past and Zeke decided to trust him. When the fighters showed up, they put on an absolute textbook demonstration. Zeke would mark the target and the fighters would hit it exactly on the mark. Both Zeke and the fighters received small arms fire, but nothing heavy. Hotel 21 sounded very satisfied and Sam was ecstatic. "Rustic, Rustic, we love you too much!"

Two days later during the Rustic daily briefing, it was announced that Hotel 21's troops had made a sweep through the school area and counted 280 North

Vietnamese soldiers "KBA" (killed by air) during Zeke's air strike. That earned him a Distinguished Flying Cross.

Target identification at night was always difficult. On dark nights with no moon, no lights on the ground, and no navigation radios, it seemed impossible. This was frequently exacerbated by haze or sometimes smoke from the annual burning of the fields to prepare them for the next crop. Dick Roberds, commander of the Night Rustics, once spent two hours trying to locate a target on one of those dark, smoky nights and finally gave up. He passed the co-ordinates to his replacements, Bill Lemke, Rustic 27, and Mick Gibbar, Rustic 25. He smiled as he headed for Bien Hoa thinking, That ought to keep those lieutenants busy for a while. Ten minutes later he heard them call with target identification and ask for fighters. "Impossible! How did they do that?"

Lemke and Gibbar flew as a paired crew for most of their tour and worked well together. Each mission, they would alternate between pilot and copilot, so each mastered all of the necessary techniques. The difficulty of night target identification bothered them, so they worked out a system based on pilotage techniques taught to all pilots, but seldom used if radar or navigational radios were available. They carried with them a pair of dividers, a Weems plotter, and an air navigation computer. The dividers allowed rapid and accurate measure-

The Mekong River as seen from the right seat of an O-2. Dave Hull photograph.

ment of distances on a map, but sometimes resulted in minor puncture wounds to the user's knee. There wasn't much room in an O-2 and the red cockpit lights didn't help. The Weems plotter was about a foot long and had half of a protractor on one edge and distance scales for aerial charts on the long edge. These scales were worthless for the one-to-fifty topographic maps the FACs carried and the plotter was too long to be used in the plane without poking the other pilot with it. They clipped the long ears of the plotter on either side of the protractor and replaced the scales with one cut from a one-to-fifty map, annotated with a ball point pen and taped to the plotter. Real high-tech stuff.

The computer was a standard E-6B model known throughout the pilot fraternity as a "confuser." One side was a circular slide rule useful for time-rate-distance problems while the back side had a compass rose and could be used to determine the effect of wind on both heading and airspeed. A few marks with a ballpoint pen made it easier to use in an O-2.

Lemke and Gibbar had already "calibrated" the O-2 and knew that at 23 inches of manifold pressure and 2,300 rpm on both engines, the O-2 had a no-wind ground speed of 4 kilometers (2.5 miles) a minute or 1 klick every fifteen seconds. Then, during lulls in the missions, they spent their time picking identifiable reference points in the area. Most of them were on or near bodies of water, as water would reflect whatever light was available and could usually be seen. They marked their reference points on their maps and gave them names to help identify them. They had points named after footballs, ducks, fish, cartoon characters, and states. During the really dull parts of a mission, they practiced going from one point to another using only their navigation system.

If they needed to locate a target, the pilot would fly to the nearest reference point while the copilot calculated the heading and distance from there to the target. He would divide the distance in kilometers by four to get the flying time in minutes and seconds to the target. The pilot would fly exactly over the reference point on the correct heading and the copilot would start his stopwatch as they passed over it.[3] The copilot would count down the time and at zero, the pilot would drop a flare and bank the plane. Voilà! There would be the target! Lemke and Gibbar figured this system was accurate up to about 50 miles (80 kilometers) or twenty minutes flying time in an O-2. It was a basically simple system, but it took a lot of practice and a certain amount of ingenuity. Lemke and Gibbar's reputation spread and, when asked how they did it, they merely smiled and looked wise. They reasoned that no one could use it if they hadn't spent the time to establish some recognizable reference points and didn't remember the basic navigation skills they had been taught in flying school.

One useful aid to target identification was the starlight scope. Basically, this was a version of the sniper scope infantry soldiers could fasten to their rifles. It was the forerunner of today's night vision goggles.

A small amount of light, perhaps from the moon or stars, entered the scope and was electronically amplified to give the viewer a good, albeit greenish, picture of what was there. The scope was sensitive to light in both the visual and infrared range, which meant that targets emitting heat, such as vehicles or humans, could be identified.

The early versions of the scope were fairly cumbersome and were held out the open window of the O-2 while the right seater looked through the other end. Because of the narrow field of view and the maneuvering of the plane, this could produce dizziness, vertigo, headaches, and even airsickness. Some of the FACs never conquered this and did not use the scope. Others weren't bothered by it and found it a useful tool when searching for some types of targets. Lemke and Gibbar used it to help locate their reference points.

The night Rustics led an upside-down life where they slept all day and worked all night. Their parties, if any, started at dawn. Because of this, they lived in a separate hooch from the day Rustics, whose parties started at sunset. The two groups seldom met, but they both used the same Intell facilities, which ran twenty-four hours a day.

Since the night Rustics had been living at Bien Hoa as Sleepytime FACs, their lifestyle was well established. Each aircrew hooch at Bien Hoa had a set of Vietnamese maids assigned to it who kept it clean and took care of the pilots' laundry and flying boots. The head maid at the Sleepytime hooch was Dung Ngoc Le, know to everyone as June. She organized the laundry and cleaning activity during the night and kept the hooch quiet during the day so the pilots could sleep. She spoke excellent English and earned the respect and appreciation of all the night Rustics.

Depending on the level of activity, the night Rustic O-2 pilots were occasionally asked to fly day missions. These were usually fragged missions scheduled the day before by Seventh Air Force to strike specific targets. These were highly cherished by the O-2 pilots as it gave them a chance to fly solo and see what the country of Cambodia really looked like. Some of these missions were flown in a "Free-Fire Zone" in eastern Cambodia. This was called "Freedom Deal" and Lon Nol had declared that territory east of the Mekong and north of Kompong Cham to be completely under enemy control. Any per-

Dung Ngoc Le (also known as "June") who was the lead hooch maid for the Night Rustics at Bien Hoa. She now lives in Virginia with her husband and two children and remains a close friend of the Rustics. Photo courtesy of Richard Roberds.

sonnel or vehicles found there were considered enemy and any targets in that area could be struck without Cambodian approval.

The Cambodian NVA headquarters was known to be located somewhere near Kratie, and Route 72 down the east side of the Mekong was a Maj. route for bringing enemy supplies deeper into Cambodia. Other FACs, particularly the Coveys, stationed in the northern part of South Vietnam at Pleiku and

Da Nang, flew missions in this area. Their primary objective was interdicting the supplies coming down the Ho Chi Minh trail to South Vietnam. They were not there to support the Cambodian army and the Mekong and Route 72 were outside their area of interest.

Dick Roberds, Rustic 21, flew several day missions trying to destroy bridges along Route 72 and cut the NVA supply line to central Cambodia. Attacking bridges was frustrating work. A bridge constructed of iron and steel required a direct hit with a bomb, which was very difficult to do. A near miss didn't do much damage.

In that era, there was nothing sophisticated about the munitions. They had no internal guidance system and their accuracy depended entirely on the skills of the pilot dropping them. The number of variables affecting a bomb's trajectory assured that direct hits were more the exception than the rule and a certain CEP (circular error probable) was established for each munition.[4] After several air strikes, Dick's bridges still stood.

In June 1971, Dick was scheduled to try it again. During the briefing, his mission was changed to fly into Cambodia and provide FAC support for a pair of F-4s who would be carrying the Pave Way System. Nobody knew what the Pave Way System was, but these new schemes showed up occasionally and nobody thought much about it.

Dick rendezvoused with the fighters on the east side of the Mekong about halfway between Kompong Cham and Kratie. The fighter leader gave Dick a set of coordinates and told him to mark it with a smoke rocket. Then he was to get out of the way and stay at 2,000 feet. The fighters would not be coming down that low.

"The first target was a bridge on the highway—one of my bridges! Were they going to take it out? I marked it and moved out of the way."

One of the fighters stated that he had a visual on the target and then repeated the words, "Pickle, pickle, pickle." The other fighter announced, "Bomb is away." For a few seconds nothing happened. Dick looked around and couldn't see the fighters anywhere. Suddenly there was a huge explosion. The shock wave rocked his O-2 and when the smoke cleared, he saw that the bridge had been lifted up and bent in half. Destroyed.

"How are you guys doing that?" The fighters didn't answer that question, but merely gave him the coordinates for the next target. Another bridge.

The same thing happened, but Dick had moved a little further away this time. The F-4s were dropping Mk-84 2,000-pound bombs with incredible accuracy. All told, the F-4s destroyed three bridges with four bombs. It would have been four bridges, but one bomb was a dud.

Dick was watching an early (and highly classified) version of a "smart bomb." One aircraft would "designate" or "illuminate" the target with a laser beam and hold it steady while the other aircraft dropped a bomb. An infrared seeking attachment on the nose of the bomb would pick up the laser and guide the bomb toward it with astonishing accuracy. At the time, this was all experimental and the F-4s were still testing the system. It worked! A year later, the Air Force would begin installing a system called "Pave Nail" on some of the OV-10s so that they could illuminate targets with a laser. Since the war in Southeast Asia, smart bombs have become very common. In Cambodia, they were brand new and the Rustics seldom worked with them.

Although never mentioned, there was a certain amount of envy of the OV-10 pilots and not just because they flew most of the daytime missions. The OV-10 had superior performance, was fully aerobatic, and just looked more like a combat airplane than the O-2 did. Most importantly, the OV-10 carried a certain amount of firepower of its own. Not much, to be sure, but enough to get the enemy's attention while waiting for some real firepower to show up. Most envied were the four M-60 machine guns the OV-10 carried. In combat, frustration was getting shot at and being unable to shoot back. The OV-10 didn't have that problem. This frustration caused a few O-2 Rustics to take matters into their own hands.

Steve Hopkins, Rustic 45, was in the right seat with an AR-15 assault rifle poked out the window. He was shooting at boats on the Mekong that were shooting at him. The technique developed for doing this was to hold the rifle upside down so that the empty shell casings ejected to the left and were caught in a helmet bag. The only rule was to always fire forward to avoid hitting your own plane.

One enemy soldier on a boat was particularly persistent with his rifle. The O-2 pilots decided to drop a flare over him and unload a full clip of bullets at him. They misjudged his position slightly and when the flare ignited, he was right under the airplane.

"Without thinking (and without the helmet bag in place) I opened up with the gun right side up. As the clip emptied, I realized I was aiming well aft instead of forward. All seemed well, however, and we resumed a normal mission and eventually returned to Bien Hoa."

After landing, they discovered several bullet holes in the right tail boom and vertical stabilizer which, they concluded, must have come from the enemy soldier on the boat.

Two days later, a maintenance officer from the Nineteenth TASS came up to Steve in the hooch and gave him a small box carefully wrapped in gift paper.

Rustic O-2 FACs at Bien Hoa, June, 1971. Standing left to right: Jack Koppin, Dick Roberds, unknown, Bob Harris, Drake Greene, Tom Jones, Ron Grattopp, Blake Lancaster, Merle Shields, Wen Pells, Don Mercer. Front row: Damon Gonzales, Wayne Baker, Mick Gibbar, Steve Hopkins, Tom Canter, Jack Bowen, Chuck Casey, Paul Dimmick. Photo courtesy of Richard Roberds.

"My troops drink Jack Daniels whiskey," he said. Steve opened the box and found two AR-15 rounds recovered from his O-2. He had come very close to shooting himself down. The maintenance officer got enough bottles of Jack Daniels to properly reward the maintenance troops who had found the bullets and quietly repaired the airplane.

Actually, the OV-10 Rustics had an unspoken admiration for the O-2 jocks as well. They were flying at night deep into hostile territory in a plane with no armor and no armament. They had no navigation aids, no long-range radios, and little hope of rescue if they went down. Nobody knew exactly where they were.

Both groups were flying the same mission and taking the same risks. The only feeling between them was one of professional respect.

Communications, Intelligence, and the Rules of Engagement

All aeronautical radios, except those in the high frequency (HF) band, are "line of sight." That means that the transmitter and receiver must be electronically visible to each other and unobstructed by the terrain. For air to ground communications, the altitude of the aircraft is an important factor. An aircraft at 25,000 feet over Phnom Penh could talk to Seventh Air Force in Saigon on either UHF or VHF radio. A Rustic FAC at 3,000 feet over Phnom Penh couldn't talk to anyone in Vietnam. Initially, the Rustics were effectively out of radio contact when they were in Cambodia. They couldn't request airstrikes from Blue Chip at Seventh Air Force (except on the OV-10 HF radio) and they couldn't explain to anyone where they were or call for help if they needed it. For technical reasons, the HF radio didn't provide instant and regular contact.

Normally, a FAC detachment included a radio operator and a complete set of radios along with a gasoline-powered generator and an antenna system. The FAC operated out of an Army landing strip and never flew out of radio contact with his base radio operator. The radio operator kept track of the FAC's location at all times and processed all air-strike requests for him. That system, which worked fine in South Vietnam, was useless in Cambodia.

The OV-10 FAC could contact Seventh Air Force because he carried a high frequency single-sideband radio in addition to four other short-range radios. The O-2 did not have HF capability and was entirely dependent on relaying messages through other aircraft.

The HF single-sideband radio was a mixed blessing because it could literally be heard around the world. Anyone with that type of radio anywhere in the world could monitor the Rustic air operation in Cambodia. Jim Lester was particularly annoyed.

"Everything we did carried a Top Secret Eyes Only classification and here we are on a classified mission and we're talking about it on a nonsecure radio system that broadcasts worldwide. That's when I said that we needed a radio relay station on Nui Ba Den."

Nui Ba Den was a 3,200 foot mountain located near Tay Ninh in South Vietnam and close to the Cambodian border. Most of central Cambodia was flat and a radio 3,200 feet in the air would actually be above the FACs and could cover most of the country. Nui Ba Den was in territory controlled by the American Twenty-fifth Infantry Division. They owned the base of the mountain, but there were Viet Cong dug into caves and tunnels on the sides of it and the Twenty-fifth couldn't flush them out.

The top of the mountain was inaccessible except by helicopter. The Twenty-fifth already had a radio station up there and it was a relatively simple matter to add some radios and a few radio operators for the Rustics.

It worked! Finally the Rustics had good communications to the rear and someone was keeping track of where they were. As it turned out, one of the early USAF radio operators on Nui Ba Den was S. Sgt. Gil Bellefeuille who later joined the Rustics as an interpreter.

> Our equipment consisted of a Mark 108 radio pallet taken from one of our jeeps and a generator. These were helicoptered onto the mountain. Living conditions were reinforced bunkers. Sometimes we were socked in by fog and we couldn't be resupplied by helicopter. When that happened, we lived on C-Rations.
>
> Essentially, we provided a radio relay to Blue Chip at Tan Son Nhut and also did flight following by logging regular operations checks with the Rustic pilots. I never fully realized what was going on until I joined the Rustics as an interpreter.

The Nui Ba Den radio station (call sign Rustic Alpha) lasted for several months. For the first two, it was the primary method of communications for the Rustics. Sometime in the fall of 1970, Seventh Air Force began testing an Airborne Command and Control Center aircraft (ABCCC) orbiting Cambodia at high altitude. The planes first used were EC-121s, which were four-engined Lockheed Super Constellations with the call sign Ethan. This call sign was later changed to Batcat or Ramrod. The planes, based at Udorn, Thailand, carried an American senior commander, a Cambodian official, a battle staff, and

Nui Ba Den (Black Virgin Mountain) near Tay Ninh in South Vietnam. Rustic Alpha (later Sundog Alpha) was the radio relay station on top of the mountain. Photo courtesy of Richard Roberds.

a full load of radios, radar, and operators. They were able to keep track of what the FACs were doing and could even monitor conversations with the Cambodian army commanders on the ground. Airstrike approval was almost instantaneous as they already knew what was going on and had the approval authority with them on the plane. Flight following and Search and Rescue (SAR) were vastly improved. When the ABCCC plane was airborne, Rustic Alpha went off the air. When the Sundog and Tilly FACs were assigned to the Rustic Task Force and began flying Rustic missions in southern and eastern Cambodia, the relay station picked up the call sign Sundog Alpha.

Another communications improvement came from Lieutenant Colonel Oum himself. He had an excellent technical background in communications equipment and had communications training in both Cambodia and the United States. When he took over at Kompong Thom and saw what radios he had been given (battery powered PRC-25 FM field radios), he set about improving their capability. Normally, the FM field radio had a very short range. Oum erected a 65 foot (20 meter) antenna on top of the tallest building in Kompong Thom and connected it to his radios. Suddenly the Rustics could talk to Oum

(Hotel 303) shortly after takeoff from Bien Hoa and Oum could contact FACs flying almost anywhere in Cambodia.

In spite of these improvements, the problem of radio transmission security was never solved. The OV-10s had the KY-28 Secure Voice equipment, which only worked between two UHF radios with the same equipment and the same daily code installed.[1] Initially, the O-2s did not have this equipment. Beginning in the spring of 1971, the KY-28 system was installed on the O-2s, but the primary battlefield radio was still the FM field radio. There was nothing secure about transmissions on that radio and anyone within range could listen in.

Call signs never changed. For the entire three years of its existence, "Rustic" meant USAF OV-10 or O-2 forward air control aircraft. "Hotel" meant Cambodian army unit or individual commander. Frequencies seldom changed either. All Rustic business with the Cambodian army was initially conducted on FM frequency 41.0.

Internal security within the Cambodian army was nonexistent. Whatever was given them in the form of code words, authentication systems, rules of engagement (ROE), procedures, or plans would be in the hands of the enemy within a day or two. This was probably because they had no adequate method of communicating among themselves. Keeping the information from the enemy was impossible.

The most frustrating problem was the difficulty of telling friend from enemy. The enemy had FM radios, spoke French, and knew the Rustic call signs and frequencies. They were capable of requesting an air strike on a friendly position or canceling one on their position.

The best solution to this was the personal voice recognition established between French-speaking backseaters and Cambodian army radio operators. The idle time spent chatting about homes and families paid off in better security. Judgment was also important. Experienced Rustics usually knew enough about the ground situation to spot a false request. Sometimes they just didn't know whether the request was legitimate or not. In such cases, they would ignore it. The risk of putting munitions on the friendlies was too great.

The early days were the most difficult. On one of my early missions in July 1970, I was flying solo as there were not enough backseaters available to cover every mission. I was patrolling the Mekong in the vicinity of Kompong Cham and not soliciting any radio contacts that I couldn't handle.

Suddenly I got a radio call from someone with the call sign of Hotel 21 Bravo, which I didn't recognize and wasn't on my list of known call signs.[2]

This wasn't unusual in those days as we were still trying to figure out who the Cambodian ground commanders were and where they were located. Hotel call signs were distributed by the senior army commanders along with the radios and the Rustics were seldom told which call signs were active and where they were located. My contact would be called a "pop up" call sign and the standing instructions were to learn as much about it as possible and brief the Intell people after landing.

In this case, Hotel 21 Bravo spoke passable English so I answered him. He told me that he was about 7 miles (12 kilometers) north of Route 7. He had about one hundred refugees, many women and children, that he was bringing down to Route 7 for transport to Skoun for relief and medical aid. Some of them were wounded and they were taking sniper fire from patches of trees on either side of their route. Could I help?

Maybe. I flew up there and found him easily. The countryside was mostly open farmland and the refugees, which were almost all women and children, were on foot. The wounded were carried on three or four jeeps. That definitely marked this group as friendly. The enemy didn't have any jeeps and didn't operate in the open like that.

Sniper fire was coming from the trees. Calling in an air strike and using bombs was out of the question. The friendlies were unprotected and bombs would injure them, too. Napalm might have helped, but it was on the no-no list that day. Not available.

I had my own guns and rockets and I used them. Hotel 21 Bravo would give me the general area where the sniper fire was coming from. I would put in a smoke rocket and, with that as a reference point, he would tell me where to put the bullets. This system was working well and the snipers were losing interest in attracting my attention. During each pass, the refugees would wave at me and I was really getting involved in the operation.

Hotel 21 Bravo asked me if I could contact his commander at Skoun and tell him what was happening. They had been out of radio range for several days.

I could do better than that. Skoun was only about 25 miles (42 kilometers) away and from my altitude of about 2,000 feet I could talk to them while orbiting the refugees. Moreover, the OV-10 had two FM radios and they could be hooked together as long as they were on different frequencies.

I had talked to the commander at Skoun before and he didn't speak English. I switched Hotel 21 Bravo to a different frequency and called Skoun on the other radio. When he answered, my plane became an electronic relay station and Hotel 21 Bravo could talk directly to him. They were absolutely amazed at this and they gabbled away in Cambodian for several minutes. Finally, Hotel 21 Bravo broke into English and asked if I could estimate where he would come out on Route 7.

Easy! I gave him the coordinates where he would hit Route 7 and he passed those to Skoun. He had no map himself, but Skoun had one and started assembling vehicles to meet the refugees.

By now, I was really caught up in this and desperately wanted to be in on the finish. Unfortunately, I was running out of fuel. One of the immutable laws of flying is that it doesn't make any difference how important what you are doing is, running out of gas will not help. I was already into my reserve fuel, so I headed for Vietnam still monitoring the radios and participating in the conversation. I never said good-bye as I didn't want the enemy to realize I was gone.

I was so short of fuel, I landed at our FOL at Tay Ninh (just inside the border) to get gas. With that problem solved, I headed for Bien Hoa. I remember thinking that this had been a pretty good day. I learned later that the vehicles had met the refugees and everyone was safe at Skoun.

Intelligence was beginning to play a significant role in Rustic operations. All of the FAC operations in South Vietnam were supporting army ground units and none of them needed their own intelligence section. The FACs attended the daily operations briefings of the unit they were supporting and depended on that unit's intelligence staff.

It was obvious right from the beginning that the Rustics needed an intelligence staff of their own. Cambodia was different from the operation in Vietnam. Initially, no one knew what was going on in that country or what the Rules of Engagement (ROE) would be. The Cambodians had no intelligence capability to speak of and almost everything Seventh Air Force knew about the situation came directly from information gathered by the Rustics.

Capt. Jim Gabel was an intelligence officer with the Third Tactical Fighter Wing (Third TFW) at Bien Hoa. When the Rustic OV-10s arrived from Tan Son Nhut, he borrowed some people from the Third TFW Intell Section (which was going out of business anyway) and some temporary duty augmentees and hastily fabricated a Rustic "Intell Hut" in the back of the intelligence section at wing headquarters. Jim provided intelligence support from there until the Rustics moved into their new operations building in mid-September.

Jim was a short cheerful workaholic who got the Intell section started and stayed with it until his tour was up. Since the flying went on twenty-four hours a day, so did the need for intelligence support. When he could, Jim would fly in the back seat of an OV-10 with one of the French-speaking pilots. Since the Rustic Alpha call sign was assigned to the Nui Ba Den relay station, he took the call sign Rustic Bravo.

In early August, 1st Lt. Don Dorr was the first Intell specialist permanently assigned to the Rustics. Jim Gabel officially joined them in early October.

In September, the Rustics took over a fighter squadron operations building right on the flight line. In there, a room about 35 feet by 20 feet became the Intell Section. They papered all four walls with 1-to-50,000 scale maps of Cambodia and that's where the crews were briefed and debriefed on their missions.

The debriefings were very comprehensive and were compiled into Daily Intelligence Summaries (DISUMs) that were sent to Seventh Air Force. The DISUMs included any problems the Rustics were having with communications or coordination. Although they were called daily summaries, each covered only a twelve-hour period, so there were two per day. Because of different levels of classification of information, there were at least two of those. This meant a minimum of four DISUMs per day. Considering the level of activity and the amount of information the Rustics were bringing back, the Intell shop was one busy place.

This Intell activity eventually created another minor problem. A security inspector pointed out that Rustic Intell room with all the maps and the DISUMs was classified Top Secret in keeping with the classification of the whole operation. While all of the pilots had Top Secret clearances, few of the backseaters did. Excluding them from the Intell section was unthinkable and they were rapidly granted "interim" Top Secret clearances without the six-month wait it usually took to obtain one.

Collecting good intelligence was one thing. Processing it and acting on it was something else. The existing intelligence system in Vietnam wasn't prepared to deal with the situation in Cambodia. This resulted in a lot of bureaucratic frustration mixed with an occasional feeling of satisfaction.

On a visit to Tan Son Nhut, Jim Gabel laid the groundwork for a scheme he had learned of through the Air Force Security Service. It was prompted by one of the Rustics reporting that he had seen an American C-47 flying patterns in Cambodia, but it wasn't firing at anything, so it wasn't a gunship, and it wouldn't answer his radio calls. Jim had previously been assigned to the USAF Security Service and had flown three missions on those aircraft during a temporary duty assignment from the Philippines. He knew that it was an EC-47 intercepting enemy radio transmissions and locating the transmitters with airborne direction finding equipment.

The way the system worked, the EC-47 crews collected data on enemy radio locations and reported it when they returned to Tan Son Nhut. Their reports were "sanitized" to disguise their source and put in the DISUMs sent to field units. By the time it got to the Rustics, the information was two days old and no longer valid. The enemy rarely stayed in one place that long. A Rustic pilot would check out the location, but there was never anything there.

Jim's plan was for the target location to be passed directly from the EC-47 to the Rustic operating in that area. The FAC could check it out immediately. The EC-47 crew would transmit the code word "Blue Beetle" on the UHF emergency frequency to alert any Rustic in the area that there was a target available. The FAC would contact the EC-47 on their frequency, use Secure Voice, and get the coordinates. In the first two days of operation, the Rustics responded to all of the "Blue Beetle" alerts and found some very good targets. In one case, the FAC arrived so fast that he found the enemy radio operator still talking on his radio right where the EC-47 said he would be.

The FACs were happy, the EC-47 crews were happy, and Jim Gabel was ecstatic. Sometimes a good idea can defeat bureaucracy and inertia.

The Rules of Engagement, or ROE for short, were literally the instructions on how to conduct the war. They included things like where and when targets could be struck, what ordnance could be used, what tactics were permissible, what minimum altitudes should be maintained, what specific target restrictions existed, and so on. The penalty for violating the current ROE ranged from being reprimanded to being grounded. For a pilot, being grounded was the ultimate penalty.

The problem was that the Cambodian operation was managed (or micromanaged) from the White House and the ROE changed depending on which way the political winds were blowing that day and who was making the decision. It was not unheard of for a Rustic FAC to takeoff under one set of rules and land five hours later to find out that they had changed and he had violated them. This was a particular problem in Cambodia, because many of the Vietnam ROE just didn't work in that situation.

The responsibility for keeping the ROE up to date and keeping the pilot briefed on them fell to the Intell section. One of the immediate problems after formation of the Rustics had to do with the new ROE then being formulated for air operations in Cambodia.

Certain river segments and roads were designated "Category A" lines of communication (LOCs). This applied to any transportation route that the Cambodians declared as outside their control and under enemy control. Any vehicles using those segments were assumed to be enemy and could be attacked without warning or clearance.

Other LOCs were "Cat B" where only motorized traffic could be attacked. One of the problems was that the maps used were hastily reprinted French maps that were many years out of date. Several well-used roads existed that were not on the maps and, consequently, were not categorized. Updating the maps and categorizing all of the roads was a never-ending problem. While this LOC categorization scheme sounded good, it ignored the fact that the local peasants were forced to use those same roads and rivers for their daily commerce. All traffic on the LOCs was not necessarily enemy traffic.

The ROE included a long list of targets that were not to be struck under any circumstances. These included hospitals, pagodas and other religious structures, and cultural monuments such as the temple ruins at Angkor.

The Rustics began carrying 35mm Pentax cameras with a telephoto lens for before-and-after pictures of targets. Jim Gabel dealt with the pagoda problem almost daily and learned an early benefit of photography.

> A Cambodian Army convoy had come under attack with the heaviest fire coming from a pagoda facing the highway. The ground commander insisted that an air strike neutralize it. This resulted in a considerable amount of radio traffic among the FAC, the ground commander, the Cambodian command post in Phnom Penh and Seventh Air Force in Saigon before Seventh reluctantly agreed to allow the FAC to put in an air strike on the pagoda. The strike was successful, the attack broken, and the Cambodian convoy was able to continue.
>
> Then the political flak started, prompted by a journalist who had witnessed the strike from the ground. The next thing we knew, the ROE were changed to say that no U.S. resources would be employed, nor would the U.S. control the employment of any other resources, against any pagoda. If the Cambodians wanted to attack one, that was solely their responsibility.
>
> Within days of this change, a FAC came back from a mission and gave me his roll of film to be developed. When I saw the pictures, I burst out laughing. He had picture after picture of rice storage sheds with PAGODA neatly painted in large letters on each roof. It had taken just a few days for the peasants in the countryside to learn and understand the new ROE.

The problem was that the Cambodians had different feelings about their pagodas than we did. We tended to treat them the same way we would treat a church or any house of worship in our country. Buddhists didn't treat theirs in quite the same way. Furthermore, they were at war and getting shot at. If the enemy was using a pagoda as a sanctuary, he had to be driven out. If that damaged or destroyed the pagoda, so be it. We have never been in that situation. If we ever are, perhaps we might feel the same way.

As the new pagoda rules took effect, another situation developed involving Hank Keese, Rustic 16. He was orbiting a pagoda near Kompong Chhnang when he noticed that all the saffron-robed "monks" had long hair. Real monks shaved their heads. These were enemy troops and Hank figured that ought to justify an air strike.

Absolutely not. Blue Chip wouldn't approve a strike on a pagoda for any reason. Capt. Kohn Om was airborne leading a flight of two Cambodian T-28s armed with napalm. He was listening on the Blue Chip frequency and recognized Hank Keese's voice, because he had flown with him a number of times. He contacted Hank and without identifying himself, told Hank he was ten minutes from the target. Hank recognized Kohn Om's voice and said nothing. Kohn Om brought his flight directly out of the sun and put eight cans of napalm on the pagoda. That destroyed the pagoda, the NVA troops and two antiaircraft gun positions.

Blue Chip asked Hank if he thought the Cambodians wanted to destroy the target. Hank replied, "I guess so. They just did!"

I personally got involved in attacking a pagoda. One day in September 1970, I headed into Cambodia and checked in with the Rustic FAC I was replacing. He asked me to go directly to Kompong Thom and contact Hotel 303, Lieutenant Colonel Oum who had recently been promoted. According to the other FAC, Hotel 303 needed some air support, and he (the FAC) didn't have enough fuel to hang around and provide it.

I "rogered" and headed up to Kompong Thom. I was going to check in there anyway, and I might as well do it first. Because of Oum's excellent English, I didn't really need the interpreter I was carrying in the rear seat, though he was one of the best we had. He did an excellent job of communicating in either English or French, so I was happy to let him do most of the talking. I made the initial contact with Oum and got his standard greeting, "Rustic-one-one-this-is-Hotel-tree-oh-tree-how-are-you-today-sur?" With that out of the way, my backseater took over the rest of the conversation.

Oum was also a very active commander. He didn't sit in the city waiting for an attack, but was constantly out a mile or so from the edge of the city looking for the NVA and making life as difficult for them as he could. Today, he was operating at a road junction about 2 Kilometers (1.24 Miles) west of Kompong Thom.

His problem was that he had a bunch of the enemy "surrounded" as he put it, in a building, but they were too well defended for him to capture. Once he gave me the coordinates of his position and the building, I could see the problem. The NVA[3] were well protected by the structure of the building and were firing out the windows and doors at anything that came within range. Unlike a Hollywood Western where John Wayne would simply gallop by on his horse and toss something nasty into a window, that didn't happen in Cambodia. No horses, for one thing. Nobody in their right mind was going to sneak up on any side of the building with the occupants possessing AK-47 assault rifles and a clear line of fire in any direction.

"We can't get in," said Oum, "but they can't get out. We think they've been using that building as a headquarters and have plenty of ammunition stored there. Rustic, I need some air support from you to take out that building."

"Roger," I said, "I'll see what I can do. What type of building is it? What is it used for?"

"Actually," he replied, "It's a pagoda, but it doesn't make any difference. I still want it destroyed because the enemy is occupying it as you can see."

It didn't look like a pagoda. It was nothing but a rectangular one-story building with a peaked roof. It wasn't even painted.

"Are you sure it's a pagoda? It doesn't look like one."

"Yes, it's actually used as a pagoda, but that's all right. I am the commander here, and I approve the selection of it as a target."

He was well aware of the pagoda problem and knew that the chances of getting an air strike on it were poor. Even with Cambodian approval, the process still had to survive the ROE and the political winds. Pagodas were almost never approved and Colonel Oum knew that just as well as I did. I told him I would try, but not to get his hopes up. He sighed and said, "Roger, Rustic One-One. Do what you can. I'm standing by."

I radioed all this to Seventh Air Force and told them, "Yes it's a pagoda according to the ground commander, but it doesn't look like one. I can confirm that he's taking fire from inside it, and he wants an air strike on that building."

Twenty minutes passed. I did some VR around the area being careful to stay within radio range of Hotel 303. Finally, much to my surprise, approval came.

"Rustic 11, this is Blue Chip. Your target is approved and we are sending you two sets of F-100s, call signs Blade 13 and Blade 17."

I called Hotel 303 with the happy news. He was ecstatic. We were going to have some serious war here.

The Huns (slang for F-100s) showed up armed strictly with Mark 82 slicks.

These were 500-pound bombs without the high drag tail fins that we liked to use near the friendly forces. These bombs had to be delivered from a fairly high dive angle and were less accurate than the high drags. Safety was not a problem since Hotel 303 had his troops dug in well away from the Pagoda. I briefed the fighters on the target, marked it, and stood back while they went to work.

Zilch. Four fighters making two passes each never once hit the damn target. They hit all around it, blew all the windows out, and probably scared the beans out of the inhabitants, but the building still stood.

Since they were out of bombs, I thanked them for their efforts and cleared them to RTB (return to base). I called Hotel 303 and told him that we really hadn't done a hell of a lot and apologized for the sorry bombing demonstration. He was philosophical.

"Rustic One-One, we thank you for your efforts. You did your best."

About that time, I got a call from Blue Chip in Saigon.

"Rustic 11, expend all of your ordnance and land as soon as possible at Tan Son Nhut."

Geez, I thought, what kind of trouble am I in now? Someone at Seventh Air Force wanted to see me badly enough to disturb my cocktail hour, dinner, and probably sleep; and he had enough clout to change my destination and make it happen. The part about expending my ordnance was a mere formality. They had some crazy rule at Seventh Air Force that aircraft landing at Tan Son Nhut had to be completely unarmed.

At that time, I had ten or twelve WP rockets left plus fourteen HE rockets and 2,000 rounds of ammunition for my guns. To expend it, I had to have an approved target. I had one, of course, the pagoda.

I spent the next half hour making repetitive passes on the pagoda, firing a couple of rockets on each pass. This took a while as the OV-10 didn't have enough power to recover all the altitude lost in a rocket pass. After about three passes, I'd have to call time out while I climbed back to a decent altitude. After firing all the rockets, I started on the machine guns. My four M-60 machine guns had only 500 rounds each, but they fired very slowly. It took about four passes to empty them.

I must say that my accuracy was a lot better than the fighters. I plunked at least half the rockets into the pagoda itself and managed to hit it with most of the bullets. That was easy since every eighth bullet was a tracer. Once you started firing, you could see where you were hitting and adjust accordingly. Although half my rockets had small HE warheads, I didn't see where I'd done much damage to the pagoda. I just didn't have enough firepower.

I said good-bye to Hotel 303. He thanked me for my efforts and told me he looked forward to working with me again and that we Rustics were the saviors of his country. He always said that. As I headed southeast toward Saigon, he and I and my backseater chatted about the war in general and our families.

All of a sudden, his voice went up about two octaves and he began shouting into his microphone.

"Rustic, Rustic, I can see it! We have the secondary explosion! The pagoda has blown up! It is on fire! I can see it! There must have been munitions stored in it and you hit them! Rustic, this is fantastic—a turning point! We are in control! Thank you, thank you, thank you!"

I turned the plane ninety degrees to the right so we could look back out the side windows. Sure enough, there was the glow of a severe fire on the horizon. It was dark, I was out of radio range, and I could no longer talk to Colonel Oum.

Because of the nature of the missions we were flying, we carried some extra recording equipment. In addition to the interpreter in the backseat, who took his own notes, I had a tape recorder sitting on the right console. It was wired into our radio system through a special plug that fit between my headset/microphone plug and the aircraft. The recorder heard everything I heard—or said. I had all of Hotel 303's comments on tape.

In addition, we all carried Pentax 35mm SLR cameras with a telephoto lens. These were for photographing targets before and after air strikes or for photographing potential targets. Before it got dark, I had several pictures of the pagoda showing it undamaged, both before and after the fighter strikes.

It took about an hour to fly to Tan Son Nhut. I landed, parked, and waited for the engines to coast down. I had a welcoming committee.

There were two blue Air Force staff cars with drivers and what I call "officious persons." These are people with some temporary authority, but no real knowledge of what was going on. Arguing with them was usually a waste of time.

One staff car was there to take my camera and film to the photo lab for instant processing. The other staff car was to take me and my backseater to Seventh Air Force headquarters. That was a short ride, and we were escorted directly to the office of the director of operations, Maj. Gen. "Moose" Hardin. Since the film hadn't caught up with us, we had a little time to clean up in the washroom and inhale a couple of soft drinks. Flying the OV-10 was a hot, smelly business. We had been flying for about four hours and we were both soaked with sweat and smelled like it. This wasn't a problem at Bien Hoa, since all the FACs smelled that way. Here at Seventh Air Force, though, everyone was wearing clean, pressed khaki uniforms, and they gave us a wide berth as we walked down the hall. After all, there were certain rules of dress to be followed in the headquarters, and it didn't include pilots wearing raunchy flying suits, sidearms, and survival vests. As Bill Mauldin put it in one of his classic WW II cartoons, these people were close enough to the war so that they didn't have to wear neckties, but not close enough to get shot at.

The developed pictures arrived, and we were ushered into General Hardin's office. General Hardin was a physically huge man and the nickname "Moose" fit him just fine. He was also one of the most gregarious, straightforward, and relaxed senior officers I had ever met. I had the pleasure of working for him a few years later when he commanded the Air Force Inspection and Safety Center.

"Wood," he said, "you Rustic FACs are doing a hell of a job—I know you are—and you got my support all the way. You cannot imagine all the heat I'm taking over hitting these damn pagodas. I'm catching it all the way back to Washington, and I gotta either show that we're doing something useful or cut you guys off. Tell me about the pagoda up by Kompong Thom."

I laid it all out for him. I showed him the pictures of the pagoda (which really didn't look like a pagoda) and played the tape of the entire conversation with Hotel 303 and the fighters. Because Hotel 303's English was so good, the backseater didn't have to translate anything.

Moose was absolutely fascinated by the tape. He was a fighter pilot himself, and I could tell that he was living the mission through our eyes.

When we got to the end where Hotel 303 described the pagoda blowing up, Moose jumped out of his chair and slammed his palms on his desk.

"That is absolutely outstanding! We've got to keep the pressure on up there, and we've got to support the Cambodians on the ground. This is wonderful. I can't wait to play this tape for some of those bureaucrats who are questioning our judgment out here."

He sat down and thought for a minute.

"However," he said, "these damn pagodas are nothing but trouble. Every time the word comes up, I start getting phone calls. Tell you what we got to do. We got to quit calling them pagodas. From now on—let's see—we'll call them—I got it—we'll call them 'large buildings.' That way, when you call in an air strike on a large building, I'll know exactly what you're talking about. If you say it needs to be hit, I'll approve it, but we won't use the word 'pagoda.' "

We saluted smartly and headed back to our airplane for the ten-minute flight to Bien Hoa. The driver of our staff car was not happy about having two smelly people in the backseat, but we didn't care. After meeting with Moose, the whole world smelled pretty good to us.

The "large building" ploy didn't fool anybody, of course, but it was nice to know we had General Hardin's support.

The pagoda problem, though, would not go away. On January 26, 1971, Don Mercer, Rustic 41, was flying an O-2 night mission near Kompong Cham with Glenn Perry, Rustic 26, in his right seat. The ground commander at Kompong Cham requested an air strike on a target that was about 1,968 feet (600 meters) northwest of a pagoda. Blue Chip approved the target and sent him a set of Cobra F-4s from Da Nang loaded with napalm. Don was well familiar with the sanctity of pagodas and was also familiar with the Cobras. In his experience, they were very accurate left and right, but tended to drop their ordnance long. He planned their run-in heading on a line perpendicular to a line between the target and the pagoda. That should take care of the target and avoid any possibility of damage to the pagoda. He emphasized the need to avoid the pagoda to the fighters. He dropped a log marker for a reference point and lit up the area with flares before he marked the target. He had the fighters confirm both the target location and the pagoda.

"Cobra Lead then succeeded against all odds and dropped two cans of napalm 600 meters short and 200 meters left of my smoke—it was a direct hit on the pagoda. The pagoda was totally consumed by fire."

The news of the damage was passed to Batcat, the ABCCC plane, and relayed to Blue Chip and Rustic operations at Bien Hoa. Apparently, that pagoda was one of thirteen on a list compiled by the Cambodians to not be damaged under any circumstances. That was not part of the ROE and no one in the Rustic organization had ever seen that list. The rumor was that General Hardin wanted Don grounded and possibly removed from flying status. Don and Glen were given the next night off so they could prepare their statements. Lt. Col. Tom Adams, the new Rustic commander, was hoping he could just keep Don in the right seat for a week or two until things cooled down and seriously considered sending him for a short "vacation" to the O-2 unit at Quan Loi.

None of that worked. On January 30, Don and his commander, Dick Roberds, were directed to report to Seventh Air Force at Tan Son Nhut. That resulted in a series of meetings with some senior officers and a complete review of the circumstances. One of the problems was that the Cobra F-4 pilot had reported that his napalm hit exactly on the smoke marker, which was not true and couldn't have been true. After reviewing facts and the ROE, the officers at Seventh Air Force concluded that Don had done everything right and restored him to full combat duty at Bien Hoa. Case closed except for a round of debriefings with the Rustic hierarchy. The ROE were the law and the Rustics were reminded that they didn't have to like them; they did have to follow them.

Sometimes, though, the ROE changes were nearly impossible to follow. The minimum altitude for FAC operations was based on the type of ground fire they expected. Cambodia was considered a fairly permissive environment as the enemy forces had only small arms, primarily AK-47 Kalishnikov assault rifles and 12.7mm antiaircraft machine guns. All were visually aimed. There were no radar tracking devices.

Against those weapons, a minimum altitude of 1,500 feet was considered safe. That did not mean absolutely safe. The actual range of those weapons was 5,000 feet or more, but it would take a lucky shot to hit a moving airplane at that distance and an even luckier shot to bring it down.

Another factor worked in the FAC's favor. The enemy knew that the FAC was capable of putting an immense amount of airpower on a target if he could identify it. Thus the enemy went out of their way to avoid attracting the FAC's attention. Shooting at him was a good way to do that. Shooting at an OV-10 was considered particularly dumb as the OV-10 carried machine guns of its own and could retaliate immediately.

Once an air strike started, the situation changed. The fighters were always vulnerable to ground fire as the enemy knew that they didn't come down to low altitude unless they intended to strike something. At that time, the FAC was also vulnerable as the enemy no longer had any reason not to shoot at him. The FAC was most vulnerable as he pulled off from a rocket-marking pass. At that point, his airspeed and altitude were both low and from the point of view of an enemy gunner behind him, he was almost a stationary target. The FACs and fighters knew this and they watched each other very closely to detect any evidence of ground fire. That brought instant retaliation.

Nevertheless, FACs did take hits. Occasionally a FAC would return with a bullet hole or two in the plane and have no idea when it happened. There hadn't been any air strikes. Someone had potted him with a lucky shot when he wasn't looking. This news was duly logged and reported in the DISUM.

After one of these events, the ROE were abruptly changed to establish 3,500 feet as the normal VR altitude with 2,500 feet as the absolute minimum.

Most FACs considered that ridiculously high as they couldn't see anything from that altitude. Many ignored it.

That caused a few problems, though, particularly on flights where the backseater was handling the camera. As Jim Gabel pointed out, it wasn't too smart to bring back pictures that were obviously taken below 2,500 feet.

Jim Lester's replacement was Lt. Col. Tom Adams, who also inherited his call sign. Tom had strong feelings about the ROE.

> We were controlled from Washington and that's one of my pet peeves. I hope we never fight a war like that again. You cannot run a war from Washington, D.C. You need a battlefield commander to run it.
>
> It's a political thing. Our FACs would bring back good, real time information, and it would be three days before anything was done about it. If Washington decided to put a B-52 strike on a target identified by the FACs, it would take three days! In three days the enemy would know about it because there were so many leaks. The leakage was such that the enemy knew exactly which areas would be hit and which areas we were not allowed to hit.
>
> As an example, on some LOCs we could fire at something if it had a motor on it and was moving. If it were a bicycle or a rowboat, you couldn't touch it. I remember on one of my early Rustic missions, I spotted a truck doing about 70 miles an hour. By the time I could get authorization from Ramrod (ABCCC) to fire, that son of a gun had made it to the next town and had pulled in under a tree. I was too late. I couldn't touch him there, and he knew it."

Eventually, the Rustics learned how their reports influenced the ROE. They were reporting what was going on and what they were doing about it. Some nonmilitary politician would read it and not understand it; and therefore not like it. Out comes a new ROE telling the Rustics to not do that anymore.

As an example of how Intell reporting influenced the ROE, in September 1970, the Rustics were flying eleven Rustic sorties a day and using a lot of air support. This increased the number of "structures destroyed" in the Bomb Damage Assessment (BDA) reports. This was a normal result of that type of combat as the enemy used structures to his advantage just as the Cambodians did. Jim Gabel, the Intell officer, started getting comments from high up and he could almost smell a new ROE coming: Don't destroy any more structures!

That's when he added a new term to the BDA lexicon; a "fortified fighting position," or FFP for short. The first time he used that in a report, he got a call from Seventh Air Force.

Tom Adams, Rustic commander, Lieou Phin Oum, Hotel 303, and Dick Roberds, Night Rustic O-2 commander, April 1971, Bien Hoa Air Base. Photo courtesy of Richard Roberds.

"What the hell's a 'fortified fighting position'?"

"Well, a 'fighting position' is usually a shallow hole hastily dug in the ground. We used to call it a foxhole. A 'fortified fighting position' is one in which the man can stand up and shoot out."

"Oh." They got the idea and the number of "structures destroyed" dropped significantly. The destruction of FFPs increased in almost direct proportion.

The Daily Intelligence Summary, or DISUM, was the single document that reported what was going on in Cambodia and what the Rustics were doing. It was compiled from the debriefings of the Rustic pilots and backseaters. It included records and results of air strikes, information passed to them by the Cambodian ground commanders, and VR information.

The DISUM was transmitted nightly by teletype to Seventh Air Force and normally ran twenty or more pages of single-spaced typing. Lt. Don Dorr ran the night shift for Rustic Intell.

The function of the night shift was to brief and debrief flight crews and post debrief information on the massive wall maps which covered every square inch of the walls of the Intell room and some of the ceiling. The big item was preparation of the DISUM covering the daily activity. This involved compiling all of the debriefs for the twelve-hour period from 0600 to 1800, editing them, typing them into official message format and transmitting them to Seventh Air Force before the deadline when the phones would start ringing if it hadn't been received. This monster document became a sinister, living thing which almost completely dominated my life.

Aircrews came in to be briefed, flew their mission, returned, were debriefed and left for the hooch where they ate, drank, partied, watched movies and slept. All that time, I slaved over the *&@#% DISUM.

With the invaluable assistance of dedicated airmen like Terry Vick, Doug Turi, and others who handled most of the briefs and debriefs, I spent night after night as editor-in-chief of the monster DISUM. Our one clerk typist spent the night pecking away on a manual typewriter to get it formatted and typed on time.

Because of the extreme sensitivity of some of the Rustic missions, the finished product usually had to be reviewed by a senior officer. I had to call this poor soul in the wee hours of the morning so that he could leave the comfort of his bed to come down to the office just to read and approve the DISUM. As long as everything was in order, I only had to pace and sweat like an expectant father while he read it. If it was not to his liking; bad news. Revisions had to be made and pages had to be retyped, all in time to meet the submission deadline.

Finally, after delivering it to the communications center for transmission, all was relatively calm again. Soon the day shift would relieve me. The chow hall would be open for breakfast and I could sneak back to the hooch for some sleep—dreaming, of course, of having to go back to the Intell shop that night and do it all over again.

In most military operations, intelligence specialists were treated like weather forecasters and viewed with a certain amount of distrust. What the hell did they know about it? In the Rustic operation, it was a partnership. The Rustics knew that they, the Rustics, were the primary source of information on Cambodia and the pre- and post-mission briefings could easily run an hour or more. Intell was taken very seriously and it was not unusual to find an off-duty pilot or backseater in the Intell shop just studying the maps or sitting with his feet on someone's desk while drinking coffee and participating in the analysis discussions.

7

Chenla I

One result of the American "invasion" of Cambodia in April was that the Khmer Rouge and North Vietnamese moved their operations away from the border and deeper into Cambodia. The Khmer Rouge moved southwest to the Phnom Santuk region of Kampong Thom Province. The North Vietnamese Army (NVA) set up their headquarters (COSVN, Central Office of South Vietnam) somewhere near Kratie. The two organizations essentially controlled the northeastern third of Cambodia with little opposition. One of their main targets was the provincial capital of Kompong Thom. They could not capture Kompong Thom, but they could keep it under siege as it had been since mid-June. The city was defended by the Cambodian Army's Tenth Brigade, which was desperately short of supplies and ammunition. The enemy wanted Kompong Thom because it was a naturally located central supply point on the routes to both Thailand in the west and Laos in the north. It was also at the northern end of Cambodia's fertile agricultural region. It was Colonel Oum's opinion that the NVA wanted both the food Cambodia could supply and a direct route to Thailand, which they planned to eventually attack. It was also Oum's opinion that, until 1972, the Khmer Rouge were not sufficiently well organized to be a serious factor. In 1970, almost all enemy forces consisted of well-trained and well-equipped NVA troops.

In early July, Lon Nol sent the Cambodian Eleventh Brigade and its acting commander, Colonel Oum, to reinforce the Tenth at Kompong Thom. The relief convoy traveled up Route 6, but even with the help of the newly formed

Rustics, they could not get past a bridge the enemy had destroyed at Kompong Thma. That was about 22 miles (35 kilometers) south of Kompong Thom and that was as close as they could get. The convoy retreated to their supply base at Skoun.

Colonel Oum tried a different approach. Exploiting their new friendship with South Vietnam, a former enemy country, twenty-five South Vietnamese helicopters were brought in to airlift the brigade directly to Kompong Thom. This tactic was successful and the enemy retreated, much to the delight of the Cambodians.

"The morale of my soldiers was very high and they were shaking hands with everybody and saying, 'We've won the war!' I told them, 'You're crazy. You've not won the war yet.' "

Colonel Oum was right. They hadn't done anything except relieve the garrison at Kompong Thom. The city was still surrounded and access to it was still blocked.

In August 1970, Lon Nol ordered a major military campaign to relieve Kompong Thom, secure the fertile rice-growing region south of it, and reopen both road and river routes to Kompong Thom. That campaign was originally called Operation Chenla Dey Teuk, which was the name of a sixth-century Cambodian kingdom. That was rapidly shortened to just Chenla. A year later when Operation Chenla II was initiated, the original Chenla was renamed Chenla I and appears that way in all the reference books. It lasted from early September to mid-December of 1970 and accounted for some of the Rustics' heaviest activity.

The first priority was reopening Route 6 from Skoun to Kompong Thom. Through most of August, Skoun was occupied by the NVA and it had to be retaken to be used as a staging base for Chenla I. Skoun was about 35 miles (57 kilometers) due north of Phnom Penh at the intersection of Route 6 and Route 7. Here, Route 6 continued north to Kompong Thom and Route 7 headed east to Kompong Cham, thus Skoun commanded a critical road junction. During the NVA occupation, they set up a single artillery gun in the door of a pagoda which faced Route 6. The pagoda protected the gun and its position provided an unobstructed field of fire. Nothing could get past it, and the Cambodian army commander wanted the pagoda and its artillery gun destroyed.

At this time, the Rules of Engagement for Cambodia were still being developed, but Seventh Air Force was pretty sure that pagodas would not be approved as targets. After several days of discussion with the Cambodians, Sev-

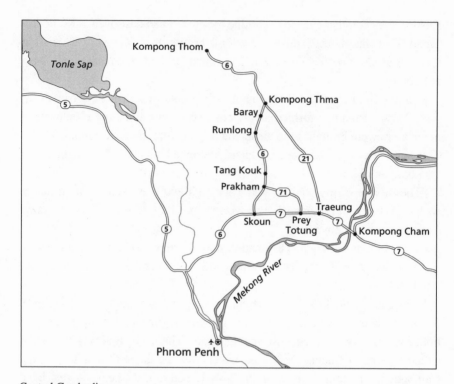

Central Cambodia.

enth Air Force finally approved an air strike on the pagoda. A Rustic FAC rendezvoused with a pair of F-100s to do the job. One of the F-100s put a can of napalm right through the front door of the pagoda and blew its roof off. The Cambodian army was once again in control of Skoun.

Skoun was also the scene of the Rustics' first encounter with news media and the weaknesses in the security of the operation.

In August, Mike Wilson, Rustic 08, was supporting a convoy that had been ambushed while trying to get through Skoun. His backseater, Walt Friedhofen, was talking to the ground commander who was requesting an air strike on the enemy positions. All of a sudden an English-speaking reporter came on the radio and asked to talk to Rustic 08. Mike had Walt tell the ground commander to get the reporter away from the radio or they couldn't put in the air strike. The reporter didn't come back on the radio, but evidently stayed close as Walt's conversation with the ground commander was translated into English and published in both *Newsweek* and *Stars and Stripes*. It was accompanied by a picture of an OV-10 flying low over the convoy. The picture was probably of Mike Wilson's plane, but it could have been any of the OV-10 Rustics. We all flew low over the convoys.

Cambodian convoys, in Jim Lester's words, looked like circus carnivals traveling to their next show. The Cambodian soldiers were poorly equipped and few of them had full uniforms. The army did not have a large supply of trucks, so they commandeered civilian busses and trucks to haul the troops and supplies. Among those commandeered were a fleet of Pepsi-Cola delivery trucks that, with their bright red, white, and blue paint, made the convoys easy to find.

Route 6 was a two-lane paved highway and the terrain was mainly open agricultural land. This was Cambodia's wet season, though, and vehicles could only move on the highway. The adjoining rice fields were flooded. The NVA technique for stopping the convoys was ridiculously simple. At night, the NVA would demolish any small bridges on the route and dig about six ditches across the highway in front of the convoy. From the air they appeared to be about three feet wide and three feet deep. The ditches only went about three-fourths of the way across the road, but they alternated. The first ditch would start from the left side, the second from the right, and so on. Thus the NVA bicycles could weave through the ditch maze, but the Cambodian vehicles could not. They were stopped until they filled in the ditches. The next night, the NVA would dig six more ditches behind the convoy so they couldn't back up either. The Cambodians learned that the first and last vehicles of any convoy had to carry road repair equipment.

Covering the convoys on Route 6 kept the Rustics busy. The fighting, though, spilled onto Route 7, which the Khmer Rouge were using for their own purposes. George Brower, an experienced Rustic OV-10 FAC, was scrambled from a sound sleep to relieve a FAC who was involved in a troops-in-contact (TIC) situation on Route 7 and was low on fuel. The fighting was near Prey Totung, a small village a few kilometers east of Skoun.

When George arrived on the scene, a set of F-100s with napalm had already been ordered. The ground commander briefed him on the situation and George could actually see some of the enemy troops. They were obviously inexperienced as some of them were casually walking down the highway in a group of about fifteen. The fighters still hadn't arrived, so George rolled in and fired a smoke rocket into the middle of the group. Those that could still move ran into what looked like a two-car garage fronting the highway.

The F-100s checked in and George wasted no time in marking the garage for them. The Huns (slang for F-100s) destroyed the garage in short order. After they left, the ground commander told George that his plane had been under

Cambodian army road convoy near Skoun, 1970. Collection of Jim Gabel.

heavy machine-gun fire the entire time. That was a surprise to George, but he quickly located the machine gun by the smoke streaming from its muzzle. He had an AC-130 gunship available and rolled in to mark the gun location for him. He must have hit a store of ammunition with the Willie Pete rocket, because the machine gun and gunner disappeared in a large explosion. The AC-130 pilot was a little miffed that he no longer had a target to shoot at.

Things appeared to be under control at that location, but another ground commander a few klicks away needed help. His troops were pinned down and taking fire from the flat roof of a two-story building across the highway. The friendlies were protected by a thick wall, but they couldn't move.

George had another set of F-100s inbound with Mk-82 high drag bombs. He briefed the fighters, cautioned them on the winds, which were quite strong, and marked the building for them. The lead fighter misjudged the wind and planted his first two bombs on the highway between the building and the friendlies. Because of the protecting wall, the only injury was to their hearing, but, as George put it, the ground commander "went ballistic." He had never been that close to an exploding bomb. The second F-100 put his bombs right on the rooftop and took care of that problem.

The friendlies were also taking fire from a tree line, so George had the F-100s use their 20mm cannon to spray the tree line. That quieted that situation down. With everything under control and most of his fuel gone, George headed back to Bien Hoa. It had been a good day and Route 7 was back under Cambodian control, at least for the time being.

Meanwhile, things were not nearly as good on Route 6. Moving the convoys past the obstacles while they were under almost constant attack was not easy.

Lt. Lou Currier, Rustic 09, was the only French-speaking Rustic OV-10 pilot at that time. Since he didn't carry an interpreter, his backseat was frequently filled with a staff officer from Seventh Air Force who needed to see what was going on, but couldn't speak French and help with the communications. Lou also gave new Rustic pilots their Cambodian checkout.

One day in early August, he was working with a ground commander in a small town north of Skoun. The commander was taking mortar fire and he knew where it was coming from. He wanted an air strike.

Lou ordered fighters and Blue Chip sent him a set of F-4s, call sign Cobra, which had been diverted due to bad weather in their original target area in North Vietnam. They were carrying a full load of Mk-82 slicks, which were 500-pound bombs without the high-drag fins installed. The fins allowed the bombs to be delivered very accurately from low altitude without endangering the fighter, but they were seldom carried by the F-4s.

None of the FACs liked to use F-4s for reasons that had little to do with the skills of the pilots. The F-4s were used mainly in North Vietnam or over the Ho Chi Minh trail in Laos where pinpoint accuracy was not absolutely necessary. Survival was, however, as they were exposed to very heavy antiaircraft fire. Their bombing tactics were much different from the close air support tactics of the fighters the FACs normally used.

To make matters worse, the F-4s carried their bombs in groups of three on ejector racks. Because the bombs were so close together at release, springs in the racks kicked two of them outward so they wouldn't collide on the way down. This meant that three bombs released from an F-4 at a reasonably high altitude (8,000 feet typically) wouldn't be close to each other when they got to the ground. In addition, the "slick" bombs they carried could not be delivered as accurately as the same bomb with high drag fins installed. Many FACs refused to let F-4s drop bombs near friendly forces.

Lou figured that he had enough distance between the friendlies and the target, so he went ahead and marked it for them. He briefed them on the location of the friendlies and specifically cautioned them to not hit the bridge that was about a klick away in the center of town. The convoy needed that bridge to get over the river.

Jim Lester was flying in the vicinity and overheard the next transmission.

"OK, lead, you're cleared in. Good bombs, lead. Two, I want you to put yours about 50 meters north of lead's hit. Got that? OK, Two, you're cleared in. Aw, S——t! You hit the f——ing bridge!"

The ground commander screamed in English, "My God, you've knocked the bridge down!" Lou went slightly berserk and told the F-4s in no uncertain terms that they were incompetent and to get their butts home. They were done for the day.

The F-4s were from Phan Rang, a fighter base near Cam Ranh Bay on the east coast of South Vietnam. By the time Jim Lester got back to Bien Hoa, his phone was already ringing. The Phan Rang wing commander was really pissed about having his fighter pilots sent home and their skills questioned. Jim was nothing if not diplomatic. He told the wing commander that the F-4 fighter pilots were really great guys and the Rustics loved working with them. The bridge thing was a minor misunderstanding that arose in the heat of combat. Case closed.

A week later, Lou was in the same area with another TIC in progress. He was still smarting from having wiped out a needed bridge, so he specifically requested A-37s armed with napalm. Blue Chip told him they were diverting a set of Cobra F-4s armed with Mk-82 slicks to his position.

"No, I won't take them."

"Yes you will."

"No, I won't. They can't hit their ass with either hand. They're no good. I don't want them. This is a TIC. Let them go spray bombs up in North Vietnam."

Unfortunately, the F-4s were already on that radio frequency and caught most of that. Jim Lester's phone was ringing again while Lou was still on his way home. This time it was a general at Seventh Air Force who wanted to court martial the FAC.

It took some fast talking to get out of that one. Jim Lester and Lou Currier flew an OV-10 to Phan Rang to try and pour oil on troubled waters. The wing commander was really surprised to discover that the FAC, who had been ordering his pilots around, was only a lieutenant. That was the nature of the FAC business, though. The FAC was there to identify the target and protect the friendlies and Lou took that responsibility very seriously. He was in charge of any air strike in his area. Jim assured the commander that Lou was one of the best FACs he had and he spoke French besides. After a lot of discussion, peace and tranquility was more or less restored. Jim, as the Rustic commander, took full responsibility and assured him that F-4s would never be sent home again.

Jim and Lou flew back to Bien Hoa. The Rustics adopted a standard procedure for F-4s, but didn't publicize it. If it was a TIC situation, the FAC would let the F-4s drop their first bombs on an empty field to see what kind of accuracy he could expect. If it was not satisfactory, he'd let them destroy the empty field and thank them very much for their work. Since the fighters never knew what the target was anyway, they didn't notice the difference and everyone was happy. Except, of course, for the ground commander. He didn't get the air strike he needed, but at least he was still alive.

During all this, the O-2 night Rustics were equally busy. Flying at night in that type of combat had a couple of advantages. As long as the O-2's lights were off, they weren't particularly vulnerable to ground fire. On the other hand, ground fire of any type was highly visible due to muzzle flashes and machine gun tracer bullets. This made suppression of ground fire easier than it was during the day.

Night combat in the O-2 could get exciting as it involved flares, log markers, tracers, gunships, fighters, near midair collisions, and the very real problem of disorientation. Occasionally, things got very tense.

Larry Landtroop, Rustic 43, was working a TIC and decided to deploy a log marker to mark the target while he waited for the fighters. The log marker would burn with an intense red flame for about thirty minutes and it would become a very useful point of reference for both the FAC and the fighters. The wire lanyard that armed the marker was about three feet long with one end attached to the aircraft and the other to the arming pin of the marker. To keep the excess lanyard from flopping around, it was coiled and taped to the marker with masking tape. When dropped, the masking tape would pull away and the marker would arm when the pin was pulled.

On this flight, the excess lanyard was taped to the marker with heavy duty nylon filament strapping tape, which Larry did not notice. When he dropped the marker, he did not see it ignite on the ground. He looked over his shoulder and there it was, flopping in the slipstream, still attached to the plane by the lanyard and the strapping tape that did not pull away.

This was not a good situation. If it ignited, it could easily burn the wing off. Larry headed for the border, declared an emergency with Ramrod (ABCCC plane), and asked for "pigeons to home plate." That stood for heading and distance to Bien Hoa. Ramrod knew Larry's location, so that information was quickly furnished. Larry explained what had happened and Ramrod vectored another plane to join in formation with him and escort him home. If bailout became necessary, the other plane would become the on-scene commander for the rescue effort.

Instructions from Bien Hoa were to jettison all remaining stores (markers, flares, and rockets). That wouldn't solve the problem, as the marker had already been dropped and was firmly attached to the plane by the lanyard. Larry jettisoned the other stores anyway.

Fortunately, as it turned out, Larry flew through some turbulence on the way back. The marker bounced up and hit the underside of the wing and then fell back to the length of the lanyard. The tape failed, the pin pulled, and the marker fell away. Larry canceled his emergency, landed at Bien Hoa, and headed directly for the bar. In retrospect, the advantages of having Ramrod available were obvious. A month earlier, Larry could have gone down and no one would have known when or where.

Even with Ramrod orbiting overhead, it was still possible for a plane to disappear without anyone knowing about it. Early on the morning of October 1,

Jim Siebold and Walt Friedhofen launched in an OV-10 to replace the night Rustic O-2. The O-2 was flown by Lt. Garrett Eddy and Lt. Mike Vrablick. Eddy's nickname was Fast Eddie, after the Paul Newman role as the pool shark in *The Hustler.* On the way, Jim contacted Fast Eddie and asked for a situation update and a PIREP (pilot weather report.) The O-2 pilots were conducting VR on Route 6 slightly north of the village of Tang Kouk. The situation was quiet and there was an overcast at 400 feet.

Approaching the area, Jim tried to contact Fast Eddie again, but there was no answer. He tried all common frequencies on three radios with no results. Walt began contacting ground commanders and asking for information. One reported that earlier he had heard a low flying aircraft near his position followed by heavy machine-gun fire. Jim flew to that location and found nothing. Walt spotted a small smoldering fire a couple of klicks northwest and steered Jim toward it. The sun was beginning to burn off the low clouds and they were not hampered by a low ceiling.

One pass over the smoke confirmed their worst fears. The wreckage of the O-2 was right next to a storage shed by a pagoda. The monks from the pagoda had laid out two bodies on what appeared to be ceremonial tables. Jim and Walt could identify Fast Eddie because of his girth and mustache, but they couldn't identify the other body. Walt was sick because he was sure the other body was Gil Bellefeuille, his longtime friend, roommate, and fellow Rustic backseater. Gil had been scheduled to fly with Fast Eddie, but he was bumped at the last minute so that Mike Vrablick could be given his area checkout. Walt didn't know that.

The next two hours were fairly hectic. A downed aircraft attracted instant response from anyone within radio range. Jim reported the situation to Ramrod and soon there were two Sandy A-1Es circling the area. Sandy was the call sign of escorts for the Air Force Jolly Green Giant (HH-3) rescue helicopters. The A-1Es were heavily armed and were authorized to do whatever was necessary to get the helicopters in and out safely. Soon there were two A-37s, an AC-119 Shadow gunship and two Cambodian army helicopters also orbiting overhead. Walt was in contact with the army ground commander and was directing Cambodian ground troops to the scene. When they arrived, they took control of the scene and helped load the bodies into the Jolly Green helicopter.

Fast Eddie and Mike had been operating under a low ceiling and were blown out of the sky by an NVA gunner using a 12.7mm antiaircraft machine gun. The 12.7mm gun fired a round almost identical in size to the American

Communist 12.7mm machine gun or anti-aircraft weapon. The gun could be mounted in pairs or fours (quad mounting) for more firepower. Claude G. Newland collection.

.50 caliber machine gun and was a deadly weapon to an aircraft flying low and slow.[1]

All available Rustics attended the memorial service at the Bien Hoa chapel. That was the first Rustic combat loss and it brought home the simple truth that air combat was not all fun and games. Sometimes the bad guys won.

Also in October, Lt. Col. Kohn Om returned to Bien Hoa to fly again with the Rustics. By now, the Rustics were well aware of his flying skills and let him do most of the flying. He also logged a few missions in the A-37 with the Rap fighter pilots. His knowledge of the situation in Cambodian was very helpful as the fighter pilots knew little more than the Rustics were able to tell them over the radio during air strikes.

There was no break in the action. Daytime sorties for the OV-10s went up to seven while the night O-2 sorties stayed fairly constant at three. Occasionally, additional aircraft had to be launched to cope with the activity. The NVA had an uncanny knack for exploiting the weaknesses of the Cambodian Army and launching attacks at unexpected locations. Intelligence brought back by the Rustics was helpful, but it was all after-the-fact; what was happening now, not what might happen tomorrow.

In South Vietnam, there was an amnesty program called Chieu Hoi. It was designed to convince Viet Cong and North Vietnamese regulars to defect and change sides. One of the methods used was a small fleet of O-2Bs that carried loudspeakers and leaflets instead of munitions. They were called "Psywar" (psychological warfare) planes and known locally as Bulls——t Bombers. They were operated by intelligence units; not FAC units. The leaflets they dropped promised amnesty and rewards and the leaflet itself was the ticket to safe defection. Those who defected were called Hoi Chanhs and taken to the Central Interrogation Center at Long Binh Army Base for debriefing. Occasionally, a Hoi Chanh would know something about NVA operations in Cambodia and Jim Gabel, the Rustic Intell officer, would be called.

Jim made several trips to Long Binh, a twenty minute drive by jeep, and participated in the interview of several Hoi Chanhs. One was an NVA major who had considerable knowledge of the location in Cambodia of COSVN, the Central Office of South Vietnam. This was the headquarters of North Vietnamese operations in South Vietnam. He was able to sketch a fairly detailed map of the area.

Jim arranged for him to be flown over the area in a Rustic O-2 to pinpoint the location. This was not a popular idea as no one wanted to take the risk or waste a sortie on a defector of uncertain loyalties. Jim Hetherington finally agreed and Larry Driskill, Rustic 35, was picked to fly the O-2. The flight took place on November 11.

The Hoi Chanh sat in the right seat and was perfectly comfortable and cooperative throughout the flight. A Vietnamese interpreter, who was also the armed guard, sat behind him and was airsick most of the flight. Aside from that, the flight went reasonably well. The Hoi Chanh was frustrated at how difficult it was to reconcile how things looked from the air with how he remembered them on the ground. He was intent on finding references and trying to communicate directly with Larry while the interpreter was busy being airsick. He picked out two areas, one southwest of the Snoul rubber plantation and the other deep in Cambodia north of the Mekong where it flowed east to west near the village of Prek Kak. This was also near Kratie where the headquarters was thought to be anyway. The Hoi Chanh couldn't positively identify the location, but thought it was probably the one near Prek Kak. He was quite distressed, Larry Driskill was disappointed, and the interpreter was miserable. All he wanted was to get back on the ground.

Based on the Hoi Chanh's efforts, Jim Gabel was able to identify two likely areas in the vicinity of Prek Kak. On November 16, he got Jim Hetherington to agree to another O-2 flight with Larry Driskill. This time, Jim Gabel (Rustic Bravo) flew in the right seat with a list of specific features he was looking for. On his original sketched map, the Hoi Chanh had marked a prominent woodpile and an old abandoned green taxi. Neither was found on the first flight.

Larry and Jim spent two and a half hours over that area with binoculars. Finally Jim found both the green taxi and the woodpile. They were under the trees, but right where the Hoi Chanh said they would be. Jim took pictures and wrote a lengthy report for Seventh Air Force requesting a fragged (preplanned) air strike on that area, preferably by B-52s.

The reply from Seventh Air Force essentially said, "Good job, but we have no other intelligence reports of enemy activity in that area. All you really have is the word of one Hoi Chanh. You need a second source before we can approve it for a strike."

As an interesting postscript, Chandler, in his book, *The Tragedy of Cambodian History,* cites comments made by Pol Pot, the Khmer Rouge leader. Pol Pot stated that by September 1970, COSVN had been moved to Kratie Province near the border with Kompong Thom Province.[2] That was just about where Hoi Chanh had said it was and where Jim Gabel confirmed it, green taxi and all. That was the second source, but it was published about twenty years too late. Sometimes the bad guys win again.

As the battle to control Route 6 continued, the Rustics lost their second aircraft. On November 23, Don Brooks and his backseater Gil Bellefeuille were shot down. Maj. Don Brooks had been the ALO (air liaison officer) for a brigade of the First Cavalry at Quan Loi and he was a very experienced OV-10 Rash FAC. Quan Loi had switched to O-2 aircraft and Don was within twenty days of ending his tour and returning to the states. He was flying out his tour as Rustic 02. S. Sgt. Gil Bellefeuille (Rustic Tango) had joined the Rustics in July after being one of the original radio operators at the relay station (Rustic Alpha) on Nui Ba Den Mountain.

The OV-10 was built for combat and could absorb a lot of battle damage. It had self-sealing fuel tanks and 300 pounds of armor plating in the cockpit. It could fly on one engine (if all external stores were jettisoned) and its flight control system was both simple and redundant. Its most vulnerable feature was probably the hydraulic reservoir and pump mounted in the cargo compartment just behind the backseat. The hydraulic system wasn't needed for flight and was turned off after the landing gear and flaps were retracted on takeoff. The reservoir was unprotected, though, and the fluid was highly flammable.

Don and Gil had the early morning "dawn patrol" flight and Gil checked in with the ground commander at Kompong Cham. The first request was to locate a missing convoy that should have arrived at Kompong Cham, but didn't. That was easy. It had been ambushed several kilometers west of Kompong Cham on Route 7 and was destroyed. Don and Gil spotted several NVA soldiers still scrounging through the debris. When they saw the OV-10, they ran into a nearby pagoda. Gil passed this information to the ground commander who began organizing a relief column to recover the remains at the ambush site. Since there was nothing for Don and Gil to do there, they worked with some other ground commanders for a couple of hours and then returned to cover the progress of the relief column. The column began taking mortar fire and asked for air support. There was a Shadow (AC-119 gunship) in the area, so Don brought him in to fire on the mortar position.

With Shadow at work, Don orbited in a lazy circle at about 3,000 feet. Several minutes later, the relief column commander told him that he could hear machine gun fire every time the plane passed over a certain village. Don flew over to take a look, but saw nothing. Ten minutes later, there was a loud explosion and the plane began to shake violently.

"Gil, we've been hit! Get ready to get out!"

"Roger that!"

Don looked in his rearview mirror and could see that the cargo compartment behind Gil was an inferno. Don headed in the direction of Kompong Cham where he knew there was an airstrip, but it was obvious that they were not going to make it. He decided to settle for ejecting over a friendly village. Don made a Mayday call on the emergency frequency and directed Gil to eject. Gil didn't hesitate at all.

Gil's ejection took off the top of the canopy and the airflow drew the fire into the cockpit. Don initiated his own ejection.

Jim Nuber (Rustic 05) and his backseater, Ron Dandeneau (Rustic Foxtrot), were to replace Don and Gil. They were just getting their Intell briefing at Bien Hoa when the word came in that Rustic 02 was down. Jim and Ron grabbed their maps and ran for their airplane. They were airborne within minutes and headed for the scene.

On the way, they coordinated with Ramrod for SAR (search and rescue) support to include Jolly Greens (HH-3 helicopters) and their Sandy escorts (A-1Es). Ramrod already had a Shadow gunship on the scene.

Both ejections were successful. Don could see that Gil had a good parachute and was going to land some distance away. He saw the OV-10 streaming fire as it crashed and then concentrated on his own landing.

Don went through the thatched roof of a barn and found himself sitting on the ground right next to a Cambodian farmer and his cow. The farmer was speechless and the cow was jumping around a lot. Don didn't speak Cambodian or French but he could pronounce the name of the friendly village he wanted to reach. He pointed in the direction he thought it was and the farmer nodded his head and pointed in the same direction. Don shed his parachute harness, grabbed his survival kit, and left while the farmer was still speechless.

When Gil ejected, he was looking down at the ejection handle between his legs instead of holding his head back against the headrest. That gave him a very stiff neck, but he was otherwise uninjured. On the way down, he forgot to release his survival kit and landed with the kit still strapped to his thighs. The kit weighed about 20 pounds and was designed to be released on a 10 foot lanyard and be out of the way during the parachute landing. Gil was knocked unconscious by the landing and injured his back because of the survival kit. When he came to, he shed his parachute harness and took his survival kit with him to a nearby tree where he crouched down and waited.

He heard troops moving toward him. He took out his .38 revolver and decided that it really wasn't much of a weapon. He didn't know whether the troops were good guys or bad guys, but as they approached they were shouting "friend, friend" in French. When he saw them and saw their ragtag uniforms and equipment, he took a chance on their being friendly. They were. They had seen him coming down in his parachute and had immediately headed for his position. He was in friendly hands.

Meanwhile, Don had left the barn and was following a trail that led in the direction of the friendly village. He decided that wasn't a good idea as they had taught him in survival school to avoid marked trails. He left the trail and hid in some grass at the base of a tree while planning his next move.

While looking around, he spotted a single individual in the shadows of some trees about 75 yards away. The individual was carrying an AK-47 assault rifle and wearing Don's flying helmet, which had come off during ejection. He was obviously looking for Don. Don slipped his .38 Special from its holster and felt that he was probably going to lose any fight with someone with an AK-47 assault rifle.

The individual was intently watching the trail and never saw Don. After what seemed like an eternity to Don, he went away.

In addition to the survival kit, all aircrew members wore survival vests that contained, among other things, two survival radios, smoke grenades, and the

.38 Special revolver. The radios operated only on UHF 243.0, which was the emergency frequency known as Guard channel. Don turned one on and immediately heard Rustic 12 (George Brower) trying to contact him. Overhead, Don could see a small aerial armada circling the area. George had been working with Vietnamese Air Force A-37s near Phnom Penh. He heard Don's Mayday call, headed for the scene, and brought the A-37s with him. Shadow was also overhead.

That made Don feel a lot better. If the guy with the AK-47 showed up again, there was enough firepower available to even the fight. George was also in contact with Gil and things were definitely looking up. George also said that the friendlies in the village had seen him go down and were sending out patrols to find him. About this time, Don saw a group of poorly equipped soldiers trotting down the trail and assumed they were friendly. They were.

All of a sudden, Don heard the distinctive whop-whop-whop sound of a Huey (UH-1 helicopter) approaching. Don waved and the door gunner saw him. On the radio, Don told George that he was being picked up by a Huey, which surprised George. He didn't know there were any in the area. As it turned out, there were two VNAF (South Vietnamese Air Force) Hueys based at Phnom Penh and there was a VNAF lieutenant on duty at Blue Chip at Seventh Air Force. When news of the shootdown came through, there was some bureaucratic delay in launching the USAF Jolly Greens. The VNAF lieutenant, without asking anyone, picked up the phone and launched the two VNAF Hueys from Phnom Penh. They both scrambled toward the scene and, since they spoke only Vietnamese, nobody knew they were there. They picked up both Don and Gil and took them to Phnom Penh escorted by a large fleet of USAF planes.

By now, Jim Nuber had arrived and heard Shadow announce that he was losing an engine and would try and make it into Phnom Penh. Jim joined up on the AC-119 and saw it streaming oil. The crew had opened up the rear doors and were throwing out everything they could including ammunition to lighten the load. The AC-119's single-engine performance was very poor and they just barely made it to Phnom Penh. With things apparently under control, Jim headed home. Jim Seibold (Rustic 13) with Walt Friedhofen (Rustic Romeo) had been launched to relieve him and had reported crossing the fence inbound and heading for the same area where Don had been shot down.

Suddenly Jim Nuber heard Jim Siebold screaming on Guard channel that he had been hit! According to Walt, there was a loud explosion in the front cockpit and the cockpit filled with dark fumes and the smell of cordite. Walt grabbed the control stick, but he could feel Jim's hands on the controls, so he knew he was still alive. He called Jim on interphone, but got no immediate answer. Jim was too busy assessing the situation to talk. Both engines were still running, the plane was still flying, and nobody was hurt.

Jim turned back toward Bien Hoa, squawked 77 on the IFF[3] and transmitted a Mayday call on Guard channel. Jim Nuber heard the call and turned back toward him, but Jim Siebold reported that there was no fire and that his plane was still flyable. Two Hawk A-37s inbound to Bien Hoa joined up in formation with the OV-10 and reported no fuel leaks or any obviously serious damage.

Jim landed at Bien Hoa from a straight-in approach with the Hawks still on his wing. Two 12.7mm rounds had entered the bottom of the cockpit just forward of Jim's left rudder pedal and left foot. This was almost the only area of the floor not protected by armor. The rounds went up through the instrument panel and exited the nose of the plane just forward of the windshield, doing a considerable amount of damage in the process.

The plane was in the hangar for almost a month being repaired.[4] When it was rolled out, the words "Captain Jim 'Magnet-Ass' Siebold" had been stenciled on the right nose landing gear door. The name didn't last long, because the Rustics had too many pilots and too few airplanes to afford the luxury of personalized planes. The nickname stuck, though, and Jim was known as "Magnet-Ass" for the rest of his tour.

Back in Cambodia, things were beginning to settle down. Don Brooks and Gil Bellefeuille were safe at Phnom Penh and all emergency situations were under control. The Cambodians were extremely grateful for all the Rustics were doing for them and were very proud of their participation in the rescue of Don and Gil, who, at Phnom Penh, were given medical treatment along with food, water, and some excellent scotch whiskey. The Cambodian Army brass wanted them to stay overnight and attend a celebration to be staged in their honor. The American embassy got wind of that and said absolutely not. The Jolly Greens were on the way to pick them up and would return them to Bien Hoa immediately. The senior flight surgeon for the Cambodian Air Force toyed with the idea of hospitalizing Don and Gil and declaring them medically unfit for travel until after the party. The embassy didn't buy that, either. American combat personnel were not supposed to be on the ground in Cambodia period. The Jolly Greens took Don and Gil back to Bien Hoa where they had their own celebration at the Rustic bar. Don was able to locate the VNAF lieutenant who had launched the rescue helicopters and made sure he attended the party. It had been a very busy day for the Rustics and Don Brooks summed up his feelings about it: "You've never lived until you've almost died. For those who fight for it, life has a flavor the protected will never know."

Prey Totung, the village on Route 7 near where Don Brooks was shot down, was under almost constant attack and changed hands several times. Prey Totung was a small village and there didn't seem to be any particular reason for the heavy fighting, but the NVA was there in strength. The fighting continued unabated on November 24 and 25. Claude Newland, Rustic 19, was scheduled for the mid-morning flight on Thanksgiving Day, November 26. The night before, he wandered over to the A-37 fighter pilot hooch to find out who was going to be on alert the next day. The A-37s kept several of their planes on alert each day. That meant that the planes were fueled, armed, and manned to launch on very short notice. "Hawk" was their call sign and the situation at Prey Totung was keeping them busy, too.

The A-37s were the Rustics' favorite fighter. They were very maneuverable and could fly slow enough to keep the FAC in sight. They carried enough fuel to have a longer loiter or play time than other fighters and they could carry a decent load of munitions. Best of all, they were very accurate. Claude talked with the pilots he expected to work with the next day. He explained the situation at Prey Totung and they discussed tactics and maneuvers to avoid ground fire, which would almost certainly be present. He also told them what support they could expect from the Cambodian army if they had to eject and gave them some ideas on how to identify them.

Claude launched the next day with George "Lunch Box" Larson (Rustic Uniform) in the backseat. George earned his nickname for his habit of carrying a sack of mess hall sandwiches with him on the flights. Claude headed for Prey Totung and got a briefing from the FAC he was replacing. The friendlies had retreated into a school complex that was located in the center of town south of Route 7. They were pinned down, but still fighting. When Claude arrived, the ground commander reported that both he and Claude's OV-10 were taking machine-gun fire from a 12.7mm gun perched on top of a four-story building in the center of town. Putting in an air strike on it was going to be difficult as it was very close to the friendly position.

Claude's request for A-37s was approved, but it would be thirty minutes before they arrived. Claude told Blue Chip that he was going to use his own ordnance to suppress the fire on the friendly position until the fighters arrived.

George Larson (Rustic Uniform) with an unidentified Rustic pilot somewhere over Cambodia. Note rockets on the left outboard pod have been expended. George Larson collection.

Claude fired several HE rockets at the rooftop location of the gun, but didn't hit it. He did suppress its fire, though, as the gunner suddenly became interested in protecting himself.

The fighters checked in, call sign Hawk. The pilots were the same ones Claude had talked with the night before. They were ready to go to work. Claude marked the target, although it was plainly visible as the biggest building in town, and explained the close proximity of the friendlies. He asked that their first bombs err slightly on the conservative side to see how this was going to work out. The A-37s did exactly that and it worked fine. George Larson was busy keeping the ground commander informed as to exactly what was going to happen and when they should get their heads down. The fighters took heavy ground fire on their first pass, but then the gun was out of business. The ground commander commented on the deafening noise of the bombs but was glad the gun was silenced.

The enemy contact was never completely broken. There was still intermittent small arms fire, which Claude tried to suppress with his machine guns and remaining rockets. The friendlies, though, were no longer under direct sustained attack. At bingo fuel (minimum fuel reserve) Claude headed for home

Prey Totung, January 1971. Richard Wood collection.

and briefed his replacement. The battle would continue, but there would be no Rustic losses that day. True to his promise, Claude got "Lunch Box" back to Bien Hoa in time for Thanksgiving dinner at the mess hall.

Several months later, Claude flew over what was left of Prey Totung. It wasn't much of a village to begin with, but now it was nothing but desolate blackened streets and empty burned-out buildings. Some days nobody wins.

A few nights later, Don Hagle, Rustic 40, was flying the last O-2 flight of the night and was scheduled to land about 6 A.M. His replacement would be the first OV-10 flight of the next day, which would arrive in the area about an hour after Don had left. Don had been working a TIC situation with the ground commander at Peam Chikang. Peam Chikang was a small village about 7.5 miles (12 kilometers) south of Prey Totung on Route 71. The ground commander and about seventy personnel were holed up in a small, walled fort on the north side of the village. They were taking sporadic mortar and machine-gun fire from an unkown number of NVA troops. From the commander's voice, he was nearly in a panic. He was losing people and the heavy fire was coming from a ditch 70 to 100 meters west of his position.

The O-2 that Don replaced had already ordered air support and a set of A-37s (Hawks) checked in with slicks and napalm. Don put in a smoke rocket about 100 meters west of the fort, but the ground commander wanted it closer and further south. Don gave the fighters a new mark and they put the napalm right on target. The slick bombs went on the machine-gun sites further south. The ground commander still reported small arms fire, so Don marked the ditch and creek and turned the Hawks loose with their mini-guns. The ground commander reported that the NVA had broken contact.

From Kompong Thom, Hotel 303 (Col. Oum) used his radio with the big antenna and called Don. He had been monitoring the action and he told Don that reinforcements would be sent from Prey Totung at first light. Don was out of rockets, flares, and fuel, so he headed home. He hoped that there would at least be a gunship who could cover the area until the first OV-10 arrived at dawn. There was none available, though, and Peam Chikang was without air cover for a little over an hour.

Don and his right seater landed with minimum fuel, debriefed, and went to bed. Later they got the bad news from Jim Lester. The fort they had defended at Peam Chikang had been overrun and all the Cambodians had been executed. The enlisted were buried alive and the officers were beheaded and their heads mounted on poles.

In addition to the battles at Prey Totung on Route 7, there was still heavy fighting on Route 6, particularly near Tang Kouk. The Cambodian call sign at that location was "Hotel 21." The radio operator was San Sok (Sam) who had been promoted to captain." All the Rustics knew Sam.

One of the last Chenla I missions was flown in an O-2 on the night of December 15. Captain Mike Davenport, Rustic 17, was flying in the right seat as an instructor and was checking out Maj. Richard Roberds, Rustic 21, the new Rustic O-2 commander. They contacted Sam and learned that he was under serious attack from a determined force of NVA troops. They had ringed three sides of Tang Kouk and their arsenal included three 12.7mm machine guns. The guns were set up in a triangular fashion, which was a common NVA tactic to better concentrate the fire on aircraft. An AC-119 Shadow gunship was on-scene, but only had 7.62mm mini-guns and could not identify the location of the NVA guns. Hotel 21 was taking heavy casualties when the guns were trained on his location.

Mike took charge and ordered air support. A flight of two F-100s, call sign Blade, was scrambled from Phu Cat Air Base with a full load of slicks (500-pound bombs) and 20mm machine guns. While waiting for the fighters, Mike worked on silencing the NVA machine guns. He instructed Shadow to orbit above him and watch for tracer fire from the guns. Mike turned on all his lights

Captain San Sok (known to all the Rustics as "Sam") the radio operator for Hotel 21, and Bill Carruthers (Rustic 34) at Tan Son Nhut, 1972. Photo by Bill Carruthers, Jr.

including the red rotating beacon and dove to mark the location of any fire. He was "trolling for fire" as the expression goes.

The fire from the NVA guns was immediate and accurate. As the tracers streaked by the O-2, Mike broke off his dive and told Dick Roberds to flip the lights off as he climbed out. Shadow was unable to spot the location of the guns. Mike did this twice more until Shadow finally saw where the fire was coming from. He fired his mini-guns, but they did not appear to have much effect. Another Shadow gunship arrived and Mike worked both of them using the same tactic for target identification. Finally, the fighters checked in and Mike quickly briefed them on the situation. By now, he knew where the guns were, so he rolled in for a blacked out marking pass. This was for real and he knew the gunners couldn't see him. His smoke rocket was right on target and the fighters were right behind him. Their bombs were also on target. Two passes by each fighter silenced all three guns.

Sam was ecstatic. He shouted that the NVA was in hasty retreat and they were running north up Route 6. Mike directed the F-100s to fire their 20mm cannon along the highway. The 20mm shell carried its own explosive charge and was an excellent weapon for close support. Since the F-100's cannon was centerline mounted, it was very accurate.

Mike Davenport's work that evening earned him a Silver Star. Dick Roberds got an unusually thorough introduction to the Rustic mission.

Shortly after that, Lon Nol ended Chenla I and declared it to be a great victory.[5] Phnom Penh celebrated the defeat of the communists. As far as the Rustics could see, there was no victory at all. Route 6 was opened temporarily, but it was an undependable route for convoys. The city of Kompong Thom was still under siege and it was being supplied primarily by small boats plying the navigable rivers and streams spawned by the Tonle Sap during the wet season. Boats, as it turned out, were harder to stop than vehicles. Cambodian ground forces were still under attack and the Rustics were as busy as ever.

On the night of January 21, supposedly in retaliation for Chenla I, an estimated one hundred NVA sappers infiltrated Pochentong airport at Phnom Penh under cover of a rocket attack. Using satchel charges, they blew up almost all of the Cambodian Air Force's airplanes. Gone was their entire fleet of Russian Migs, French Magisters, and most of their helicopters. Also destroyed was Cambodia's national airline. Air Camboge had only a single plane, a French Caravelle that was a twin-engine medium-range jet transport. By dawn it was a burned-out hulk.

Don Mercer was there in an O-2 with Larry Landtroop in the right seat. They were working a TIC situation at a small village about 9 miles (15 kilometers) north of Phnom Penh. They were running blacked out and using a Shadow gunship to suppress some 12.7mm gun sites. Suddenly, they saw rockets rising from the ground between them and Phnom Penh. A tremendous explosion lit up the horizon. They could feel a slight buffet from the shock wave as they headed toward Phnom Penh, bringing the Shadow gunship with them. It was obvious that Pochentong airport was under attack from rockets, mortars, and munitions, which they later learned were satchel charges set off by NVA sappers. Secondary explosions, probably from the ammo dump and the fuel storage area, were going off continuously. An A-37 Hawk flight armed with CBU[6] had been scramble from Bien Hoa and was on frequency waiting for instructions.

There were broken clouds at about 1,000 feet, which made the rocket launching sites difficult to pinpoint. They were about to return to Bien Hoa because of low fuel when another set of 122mm rockets was launched from east of Phnom Penh. Here, there were fewer clouds and Don was able mark the sites where he had seen the rockets launched. He marked four other sites and received intense 12.7mm AA fire from each of them. Don's replacement, Bob Messer, arrived and diverted the A-37s originally meant for the TIC north of Phnom Penh. Two more Shadow gunships showed up as Seventh Air Force had obviously gotten the word about what was happening at Phnom Penh. Bob Messer took over and began using them on the rocket launch sites and gun emplacements.

Now Don and Larry were definitely short of fuel. Normally, they would have declared an emergency and landed at Phnom Penh, but that was out of the question. They headed for home and discussed all fuel conservation methods including jettisoning rocket pods and landing at Tay Ninh, just inside the Vietnam border. They made it to Bien Hoa "on the fumes" so to speak. Later, a crew chief told Don that he had pumped 108 gallons of gas into the O-2, which had a capacity of 110 gallons. Normally, there were at least two gallons of unusable fuel, so they were really running on the fumes.

The debriefing took four hours and Don and Larry were totally frustrated and exasperated at how little they were actually able to do about the attack at Pochentong Airport.

After the attack, the Cambodian people in Phnom Penh suddenly realized that Chenla I was not a victory at all, and they began to lose faith in Lon Nol. In February he suffered a major stroke and was evacuated to an American hospital in Hawaii for recuperation.

Also in February the Rustics lost their commander, Jim Lester. His tour was up and there were no extensions. In a little over seven months he had built an organization from scratch and left behind a fully operational unit manned with experienced FACs and interpreters.

His replacement was Lt. Col. Tom Adams. Tom was an O-2 FAC operating in I Corps near the border with North Vietnam. He was assigned as the Rustic commander and given an OV-10 checkout at Da Nang before he left for Bien Hoa.

River Convoys

When Tom Adams took over as Rustic commander, he inherited the problem of both officers and enlisted men living in the Rustic hooch. Jim Lester had this under control and everything had seemed to be working well, at least as far as the Rustics were concerned.

This time, the opposition was not coming from the base commander. It was coming from other units on the base whose enlisted men resented the idea that the Rustic enlisted men were living with the officers.

All military services in the United States and probably throughout the world have strong policies against fraternization, the mixing of officer and enlisted ranks. This separation of living and eating facilities is strictly maintained even under difficult circumstances such as on Navy submarines. This was not related so much to the privileges of being an officer, as to the rights of the enlisted ranks to live their off-duty lives as they chose and not the way the officers chose. Enlisted men understood this and generally had no interest in mingling socially with the officers, much less living and eating with them. In general, the policy was a good one and it worked fine in large military organizations. As the size of the organization got smaller, the benefits of non-fraternization also got smaller, and sometimes it became more of a hindrance than a help. A two-man flight crew with one officer pilot and one enlisted interpreter was a good example of a situation where the policy didn't work very well. In addition to the security requirements, the job demanded a lot of trust and cooperation that came from learning each other's habits, skills and techniques. The Rustics were quite happy with the team spirit established between the pilots and the backseaters.

Nevertheless, other enlisted personnel at Bien Hoa knew what was going on with the Rustics and did not like it. The Rustic backseaters were aware of the complaints. They knew the Rustic commander would eventually have to move them out of the Rustic hooch even before he knew it. The enlisted backseaters held an informal meeting of their own and decided, out of respect for the pilots, that they would go graciously and without complaint.

Thus while Tom Adams expected some really bad feelings, they came primarily from Capt. Clint Murphy, who was an interpreter himself and the officer-in-charge (OIC) of the backseaters. Some said this was an expected reaction and others said it was because Clint couldn't move out with them. Clint was absolutely loyal to the other backseaters, but the nonfraternization rule worked both ways.

By now, Bien Hoa had designated one hooch in the officer flight crew area to be used by all enlisted aircrew members of all units and the Rustic backseaters were moved there in May 1971. It was only two hooches away from the Rustic hooch, so it wasn't much of a move. The Rustic backseaters still hung out at the Rustic bar, so it wasn't much of a change, either.

Tom Adams' first operational problem cropped up in January 1971, shortly after he took over. Cambodia was slowly starving to death. By January 1971, the NVA had blocked Route 4, which was the lifeline between Phnom Penh and Kompong Som, Cambodia's only seaport and oil refinery. The NVA blocked the highway at Pich Nil Pass where it passed through the Elephant Mountains about 62 miles (100 kilometers) southwest of Phnom Penh. It was a natural ambush point and there was no satisfactory way around it. Even with Rustic support, a truck convoy could not make it through the pass without coming under attack. A destroyed truck would block the pass to all traffic for days.

In addition, there was still fighting in the Kompong Thom area and Route 6 was by no means secure. This had severely reduced the agricultural output of the central region. Cambodia was running short of both food and fuel.

The United States attempted to provide some relief to Phnom Penh's increasingly isolated population by sending in supplies on C-130 and C-141 transports. The amount of supplies they could carry was a fraction of what Phnom Penh needed and the NVA's periodic shelling of Pochentong Airport made this a risky operation. With no American troops on the ground to defend it, the airport was considered insecure and a USAF transport destroyed on the ground in Cambodia would be hard for the White House to explain.

Basically, the U.S. air support of Cambodia did not include troops, military assistance, or massive amounts of supplies. The U.S. Embassy in Phnom Penh was severely limited on personnel, activities, and the supplies and equipment they could bring into Cambodia.[1]

The decision was made to resupply Cambodia using ship convoys on the Mekong River. The Mekong was navigable by ocean freighters as far as Phnom Penh, where there was a turning basin. Since the Mekong delta was in South Vietnam, using the river was never an option until Lon Nol overthrew Sihanouk, and Cambodia and South Vietnam began cooperating in their mutual struggle against the North Vietnamese. These river convoys provided yet another mission for the Rustics; flying combat air patrol over the convoys during the entire time they were inside Cambodia. The ships, naturally, were inviting targets for the NVA. A large ship sunk in a narrow part of the channel would close down the entire resupply operation.

Tom Adams was brought into the initial planning for this since he was providing most of the air cover. The Tilly FACs were close enough to provide cover for the initial part of the convoy's trip, Tom and his deputy commander for OV-10 Operations, Maj. Bob Clifford, flew an OV-10 to Binh Thuy in the delta region where they met with an Army general and a Navy admiral.

The Army general tried to impress on Tom the importance of convoy protection. "This is going to take your entire effort. We need everything you have. This is Priority One!"

"General," Tom replied, "our whole mission is Priority One. There can't be two Priority Ones."

That, as Tom quickly learned, was not the answer the general expected or wanted. After much discussion, Tom allowed that while it would stretch him a little thin, he could give the general top priority and still cover his other missions. Based on the planning, Tom didn't think that the convoy scheme was likely to consume a lot of his resources.

He was right. The convoy schedule was classified Top Secret and Tom would suddenly get a cryptic message that decoded as, "Convoy starting." He soon learned not to panic and launch extra FACs to cover it. The convoys seldom started on time and when they did, they moved roughly at the speed of a brisk walk. Whichever Rustic FAC happened to be airborne could check on the convoy to see if it had actually started yet. Once it moved, the Rustics had nearly a full day to organize coverage before the convoy reached enemy territory in Cambodia.

The first convoy moved up the Mekong toward Phnom Penh on January 17, 1971. It was a forty-five-vessel South Vietnamese convoy consisting of ocean-going cargo ships and large barges. It was managed by representatives from the armies and navies of the United States, South Vietnam, and Cambodia.[2] Six different organizations were involved, not counting the Rustics, and it was predictably difficult to determine who was actually in charge.

The first Rustic convoy cover was flown by Capt. Hank Keese, Rustic 16. Hank spoke French and didn't carry an interpreter, but that wasn't any help. He couldn't talk to the convoy on any of the frequencies he had been given. He VR'd ahead of the convoy and picked out two spots on tight river bends where enemy attack could be expected. Unfortunately, he couldn't get Blue Chip to approve preemptive airstrikes even though there were no friendly troops in the area and no civilian population centers nearby.

As Hank ran low on fuel, he was replaced by Lt. Jim Nuber. Hank showed Jim the "hot spots" and mentioned the difficulty in talking to the convoy and getting clearance for air support.

Hank's analysis turned out to be exactly correct. The convoy came under fire at the predicted points and Jim obtained air support only by telling Ramrod (ABCCC airplane) that he had Seventh Air Force approval, which he did not. He put in several sets of fighters and the convoy finally made it through to Phnom Penh, but not without losses. Because of the near-disaster with that first convoy, Hank and Jim were invited (ordered, actually) to a debriefing session on a Navy barge near Binh Thuy.

Hank and Jim flew an OV-10 to Binh Thuy and were helicoptered to the Navy barge anchored in the middle of the Mekong. This meeting involved generals and admirals from all three countries. This was a little intimidating for an Air Force captain and a lieutenant. A U.S. Navy admiral gave an overview of the convoy operation and asked Hank what had happened. Hank described the difficulties in talking to the convoy, the location of the "hot spots" he had found, and the lack of air support. Jim took over and explained how he had precoordinated everything with the nearby Cambodian ground commanders and the province chiefs and how he had attacked the enemy with fighters without having any real clearance to do so. The generals and admirals already knew the results of that and knew that Jim's actions were probably the only reason the convoy made it to Phnom Penh.

What, they wanted to know, would it take to get the convoys through with less risk of attack? That was easy. They had to understand how the FAC did his job; how he coordinated with all the players, identified targets, and managed the fighters. They had to trust the FAC to know what was going on and give him what he asked for. Waiting for the ships to come under attack and then requesting airstrikes was dumb! The ships couldn't take cover. The air support should already be there. The FAC was the only one likely to know when and where it would be needed.

They agreed. Convoy operational procedures improved immediately and air strikes requested to defend a convoy got high priority attention. Cambodian navy personnel, both officers and radio operators, were sent to Bien Hoa for training on how to work with the FACs. Since they didn't speak English, the class was organized and taught in French by the Rustic backseaters who, by now, were experts on teaching these subjects. They were the ones who would be talking to the Cambodians aboard the ships. This was a well-organized training course complete with lectures, handouts, and a test. The Rustics saw a dramatic improvement following the graduation of the first class. From then on, each ship in a convoy carried a Cambodian officer and a radio operator who could work directly with the Rustic overhead. The Rustics also made another set of lifelong friends in the Cambodian navy.

Eventually, convoy protection involved a lot of different organizations. Both Cambodian and South Vietnamese Air Forces participated. The U.S. Navy used their "Black Pony" OV-10s[3] and the Army used helicopter gunships. In addition to the Rustics, both Tilly and Sundog FACs were involved and gunships were used for protection at night. Air strike fighters were brought in as necessary.

Once the procedures were established and the people trained, convoy patrol became fairly routine and turned out to be one of the Rustics' most tedious and boring missions. Most of the time, nothing was happening and there was nothing to do except fly around and study the terrain. This was particularly true during the wet season. Then, the Mekong would overflow its banks, which effectively widened the river and denied the NVA any close access to the convoy.

Boredom is a bad thing in any airplane and it is particularly bad in a combat environment where the pilot is mentally in a war-fighting mood. Sometimes boredom translates into mischief. Walt Friedhofen (Rustic Romeo) flew a convoy cover mission with a fairly new Rustic pilot during the flooded wet season. To liven things up (and probably keep himself awake) the pilot put on an aerial display for the convoy consisting of low level aerobatics. The display, as the expression goes, "watered their eyes." The convoy commander reported that everyone on all fifteen ships was watching from the starboard rail and cheering wildly. He was particularly impressed with the waterspout the OV-10 was kicking up as it passed the command boat. That's *low!* Walt had as much flying time as any of the backseaters, but he had never ridden through anything like that. When he got back to Bien Hoa, he managed to calm down with the assistance of several beers.

In the dry season, though, the river narrowed, the bends got sharper, and enemy could move freely about the surrounding countryside and operate in the foliage along the riverbanks. That kept the Rustics busier and cut down on the air shows. Sometimes the activity got pretty exciting. In May, Jim Nuber was capping a convoy when it came under attack just short of the final bend in the river before Phnom Penh. One of the barges was loaded with explosives, which Jim thought were probably 500-pound Mk 82 bombs. Naturally, that barge came under attack. Jim had a flight of A-37s on station and cleared one

Rustic backseaters proudly wearing their newly awarded aircrew wings, June 1971. Standing, left to right: Walt Friedhofen, Bob Montmarquet, George Larson, Emil Brunelle. Kneeling: Pierre Ligondè, Joe Paquin. Clint Murphy Collection.

in hot just as the barge took a hit. and erupted in a spectacular explosion. The A-37 pulled off his target just in time to avoid shrapnel from the blast. The rest of convoy made it to Phnom Penh, minus the munitions barge.

By the summer of 1971, attempts to keep convoy, movements secret had become a joke. One convoy in July was getting daily coverage from the *Stars and Stripes*[4] and it was so accurate that the newspaper must have had a reporter and a radio on one of the ships. Steve Hopkins, Rustic 45, capped that convoy, which was taking continuous heavy fire from along the river banks. He used several flights of A-37 fighters along with gunships on the heaviest concentrations of fire. At least four Rustics helped with the air strikes. Finally, by late afternoon, the lead ships reached a relatively friendly part of the river just south of Phnom Penh. The battle went on throughout the night and into the next day before the last ship made it to the dock.

The next day's issue of *Stars and Stripes* had a banner headline reading, "Convoy Arrives," and a picture of the first ship unloading its cargo. The cargo turned out to be about two hundred Honda motor scooters for the local dealer. Instead of the food, medicine, fuel, and munitions that the Rustics assumed was on the convoy, almost the entire cargo was commercial goods. In Steve Hopkins' words, "We were really pissed! The only good news was that we hadn't lost anyone."

From then on, it was very difficult to get a Rustic to take any unusual risks to protect a convoy. Nevertheless, combat air patrol (CAP) of Mekong River convoys became a permanent part of the Rustic mission.

The summer of that year brought another milestone for the Rustics. On June 5, 1971, a special message from the USAF chief of staff ordered the immediate recognition of all Rustic backseaters as combat crew members and awarded aircrew member wings to all backseaters who had flown more than ten combat missions—which was all of them. Recognition had finally arrived, just under a year after the first enlisted interpreter was strapped into the backseat of an OV-10 to fly the first of many combat missions. The pride of the backseaters as their wings were pinned on was only slightly greater than the pride of the Rustic pilots who watched. The war was temporarily canceled (or so it seemed) as the celebration of that occasion suddenly took precedence. One of the universal truths in any society is that recognition of achievement is the strongest form of motivation.

Chenla II

In the summer of 1971, Col. Lieou Phin Oum was still in charge of the brigade at Kompong Thom. In spite of the failure of Chenla I, he had moved his security perimeter to nearly 5 miles (8 kilometers) around the city and he had used a paved section of Route 6 north of the city to build an airport. With no concrete, asphalt, or equipment, he used whatever he had to construct the runway shoulders and taxiway. Paving was done with bricks from destroyed houses and smoothed with a GMC truck loaded with forty people for extra weight. Although the Rustics never used this runway, Cambodian C-47s used it to bring in supplies.

There was still no highway access to the city and supplies had always been a problem. Initially, Cambodian C-47s and USAF C-130s were used for airdrops. The C-47s dropped from a fairly high altitude and were very inaccurate. Oum estimated that half of those supplies went to the enemy. C-130s, using their low altitude extraction technique, could put a load of supplies right where Oum wanted it. "We didn't even have to go out and collect the supplies. They dropped them right in front of the warehouse!"

Next, water convoys using small boats were used. The boats were loaded at Kompong Chhnang and sailed across the Tonle Sap and up the Stung Sen River west of Kompong Thom. As part of their daily operations, the Rustics provided air cover for these convoys. With the expanded security perimeter and regular supplies by air and boat, life at Kompong Thom returned to something approaching normalcy.

Colonel Oum's brigade strength was about thirteen hundred troops. All of them were volunteers and ranged in age from sixteen to forty. Many came from Phnom Penh, but Oum was very successful in recruiting along Route 6 near his mother's hometown of Rumlong. "Along there, I knew everyone from Tang Kouk to Baray." (See map of central Cambodia in Chapter 7.)

In Cambodian society, the family followed the soldier. Thus one recruit might bring with him his wife, father, mother, and children, who carried supplies and cooked for the soldier. Thus the total size of Oum's brigade was around thirty-five hundred people.

His initial military equipment came from the supplies the NVA (and Chinese) had been shipping to Kompong Som for transport to South Vietnam. When Lon Nol took over, he closed down this supply route and confiscated the supplies then in transit. The supplies airdropped by USAF C-130s were arranged by the American Embassy in Phnom Penh and the Rustics would make an occasional contribution of captured arms and munitions obtained through military sources in South Vietnam.

During the summer of 1971, Oum made several trips to Bien Hoa to pick up arms and deliver Cambodians who were to train with the Rustics. Occasionally, his cargo would include a gift for the Rustics, some bottles of "Bayon Brew," a very potent rice beer from the brewery at Kompong Som. As Lt. Lansford (Lanny) Trapp was the designated hooch honcho, or house mother, the bottles were stored in his room. Once, after a hot bumpy trip from Cambodia, the bottles began exploding and thoroughly soaked Lanny's room. Once chilled, Bayon Brew was a very good beer.

One trip, Oum brought the Cambodian National Ballet, who put on a performance of Cambodian national dances at a theater in Saigon. Many Rustics attended both the performance and the following reception at the Tan Son Nhut Officer's Club. The Rustic enlisted backseaters were not invited until someone pointed out that they were the only ones who could talk to the ballet troupe. They wore civilian clothes and were introduced as interpreters. Only the Rustics knew they weren't civilians and weren't officers.

Lon Nol recovered from his stroke and returned to Phnom Penh in April of 1971. Based on his misconception of the success of Chenla I, he began planning a second major offensive to be called Chenla II. The objectives would be similar but more ambitious than those of Chenla I. The first objective was to open the highways to Kompong Thom from both Skoun and Kompong Cham. Second was to stop the flow of enemy supplies from the northeast to the Kompong Chhnang region at the southern end of the Tonle Sap. Third was to regain control of the central agricultural region. The Rustics didn't see much difference between those objectives and those of the Chenla I operation in 1970. They would be fighting for the same real estate that was supposedly captured during Chenla I. The Cambodian army general staff feared that Chenla II would expose the army's flanks and provide an easy target for the NVA. Lon Nol's attitude was that U.S. airpower would prevent any such disaster.[1] This showed a serious lack of understanding of what airpower could and could not do. Airpower could not occupy and control territory.

Chenla II started with a reported twenty thousand Cambodian troops committed, but that figure was heavily inflated. The problem was the Cambodian method of recruitment. Commanders were expected to recruit their own troops, which led to rampant corruption. According to Oum, if someone told the Army that he could raise a battalion, the Army said "OK" and made him a colonel. He would then report nonexistent soldiers and receive pay and supplies for them. The money went to the corrupt officers and the supplies including weapons, munitions, rations, and medicine, went to the black market and found their way to the NVA. "Sometimes," according to Oum, "a battalion would actually only have one company instead of three and the company would only have fifteen soldiers instead of three hundred. Army headquarters could not understand how a company that supposedly had three hundred soldiers could be overrun by a platoon-sized enemy force."

The reason they couldn't understand it was because the army general staff in Phnom Penh would never go into the field and see what was actually going on. Since the Rustics worked with all the field commanders, they had a good idea of who was honest and who was padding the numbers. They could make a rough estimate of how many soldiers actually existed by just flying over them and looking. If a commander was going to lie about the strength of his force, he also had to lie about what they were doing. This was particularly evident in the bomb damage assessments (BDA) they reported to the Rustics after an air strike. The pilots could usually make a good estimate of the results of an air strike based on the accuracy and the number of secondary explosions. They would always ask the ground commander for his BDA when it was available. If the ground commander came back immediately with a large KBA (killed by air) figure rounded to the even hundreds, the Rustic pilot knew it was padded. He would report it at the Intell debriefing, but add his opinions to go with it.

Colonel Oum would almost never give the pilot a BDA immediately after an air strike. He didn't know the exact results and wouldn't pass any on until he found out what they were. That might take him until the next day and he would pass yesterday's BDA to whichever Rustic was overhead. If he said there were twenty-seven enemy KBA it was because he had personally gone out and counted twenty-seven bodies. If he said his present strength was 1,250 soldiers, that was 1,250 troops trained, equipped, and available. He was scrupulously honest and he exposed dishonesty and corruption when ever he found it. That kept him in chronic trouble with the army headquarters in Phnom Penh and eventually led to his reassignment to the Cambodian embassy in Thailand.[2]

Lt. Col. Kohn Om continued leading the Cambodian T-28s on close air support missions. He kept in close contact with the Rustics on their radio frequencies and the Rustics treated him as another available fighter resource, one who could attack targets without waiting for anyone's permission. Doing this with the assistance of the Rustics was a technical violation of the ROE, but nobody complained. The Rustics were there to support the Cambodian Army and they weren't fussy about where the support came from. As a pilot, Om was as well qualified as any other available fighter pilot and it was, after all, his country.

In November 1971, Kohn Om missed the last part of Chenla II as he was sent to the United States for nearly a year of advanced training. This included training in academic instruction, special operations, counterinsurgency, and squadron operations. While he was there, he managed to visit his good friend and former Rustic Commander, Lt. Col. Jim Lester, at his home in Florida.

Chenla II officially began on August 20, 1971, with the Cambodian army fighting their way up Route 6 from Tang Kouk and arriving at Kompong Thma on September 1. Colonel Oum's brigade pushed south from Kompong Thom and linked up with the main column on October 5. They met approximately 15 miles (25 kilometers) south of Kompong Thom with the Rustics providing air support to both units.

Based on that link-up, Lon Nol declared the first phase of Chenla II a success and ordered his troops to stand down in preparation for the second phase; the pacification of the local population.[3]

Meanwhile, another unit of the Cambodian army attempted to fight their way up Route 21 from Kompong Cham while units from Kompong Thma, now established on Route 21 south of Kompong Thom, attempted to move down Route 21 to meet them. Neither group made much progress and Route 21 between Traeung and Kompong Thma stayed in NVA hands.

Lt. Col. Kohn Om, commander of the Cambodian T-28
"Scorpions" during a visit to the Rustics at Bien Hoa, 1971.
Walt Friedhofen collection.

On September 26, while supporting the battalion moving north up Route 21
from Traeung, the Rustics lost another aircraft. Lt. Lanny Trapp, Rustic 07
and his Cambodian backseater, Sergeant Khorn, were shot down.

Lanny was supporting Hotel 05 north of Kompong Cham. Hotel 05 had a
TIC situation and was taking heavy fire. Lanny was working with Hawk A-37s
from Bien Hoa when Sergeant Khorn told him they were being shot at. Lanny
could see the tracers coming by the aircraft, which meant it was probably from
12.7mm antiaircraft machine guns.

The guns were out in the open and easy to spot, so Lanny marked them with a smoke rocket and cleared one of the fighters in with a Mk 82 bomb. The bomb hit close to the marker, but it was a dud. Next, the fighter used his rockets and was able to shut down one of the guns. Lanny was orbiting at about 3,500 feet when he suddenly noticed that his left wing was on fire. He called Mayday over the radio and headed for Kompong Cham, which was considered friendly territory. Based on the Mayday call, Jolly Green rescue helicopters launched immediately from South Vietnam.

Lanny saw that most of his left wing outboard of the engine was gone and the plane was getting very hard to fly. It took full right aileron and full right rudder to keep it upright. They were nearly over Kompong Cham when he ordered Sergeant Khorn to eject. Lanny ejected right behind him, but to do so he had to release the aileron and rudder pressure he was holding. The plane rolled violently to the left and Lanny estimated that he ejected horizontally at about 2,000 feet. He remembers the air being filled with one-to-fifty scale maps from his map bag. The OV-10 crashed into the Mekong and Lanny and Sergeant Khorn landed uninjured in the middle of town. They were immediately "rescued" by the townspeople, who treated them as heroes. Within a few minutes, the Jolly Greens arrived and took them to Bien Hoa.

Their "debriefing" took place in the Rustic bar and was probably one of the last serious parties held there.[4] The Rustics were packing to leave Bien Hoa and move to Ubon.

Three days after the Lanny Trapp shootdown, Seventh Air Force found a new job for the Rustics. About midnight, Lt. Ron Van Kirk heard a knock on his door and found himself facing the Rustic OV-10 commander, Maj. Bob Clifford.

"We need three volunteers for a mission. They have to be single."

"Wait a minute. There are only three single Rustics in this whole outfit!"

"That's true."

"In that case, I guess I'm a volunteer. What's the mission?" Maj. Clifford really didn't know the details, but told Ron to be at the flight line at 0600 hours in the morning with whatever he needed to live somewhere else for a couple of days. The mission would be explained at that time. Ron went back to bed and slept; but not very much.

At 0600, Ron met with the other single "volunteers," Otto Walinski and Bob Berry. There was a group of marines and some other people they had never seen before. Bob Clifford was also there.

There was a major offensive by the Viet Cong to capture Tay Ninh, a South

Cambodian Sergeant Khorn and Lt. Lanny Trapp "debriefing" at the Rustic bar after being shot down and rescued near Kompong Cham, September 1971. Ron Van Kirk collection.

Vietnamese Provincial Capital, and Krek, a besieged town in Cambodia, about 30 miles (48 kilometers) up the highway from Tay Ninh. The three volunteers were to be "inserted" with Army and Marine units at Tay Ninh East, Tay Ninh West and Katum, about 25 miles (40 kilometers) north of Tay Ninh. Their job was to call in air strikes as needed to halt the enemy offensive. They drew straws and Otto got Katum, Bob got Tay Ninh East, and Ron went to Tay Ninh west. The Marines were assigned to protect them and would be with them the entire time. They were issued AR-15 assault rifles and loaded onto helicopters for the trip.

Nonpilots tend to think that combat flying is highly dangerous. In some cases it is, but pilots are very comfortable in that environment and are doing something they are well trained to do. Danger, to them, is being removed from the friendly confines of an aircraft cockpit, issued an AR-15, and planted on the ground with the real troops.

The Army commander at Tay Ninh West was a little surprised when Ron showed up, but he installed a complete set of radios in the headquarters compound and put Ron in business just a few feet from his door. It was soon obvious why Ron was needed. The army personnel there knew nothing of Air Force ordnance, safe separation distance, FAC and fighter procedures or selection of targets. Ron gave the commander a quick lesson on those subjects and they developed a plan where the commander would identify the threat and Ron would explain his air support options to him. It worked very well. Bien Hoa was close enough to furnish "on demand" air support. After four days, the enemy offensive had been blunted and the commander agreed that he no longer needed Ron. He now both understood and appreciated air support. The Marines got Ron a ride on a Huey (UH-1 helicopter) that was headed for Long Binh army base near Bien Hoa.

It was dark at Bien Hoa and the helicopter pilot didn't bother contacting the control tower or using the airfield. He just found an open area near the perimeter fence and landed to let Ron off. It turned out that he had dropped Ron in a minefield separating the ARVN and USAF sections of Bien Hoa. Ron tiptoed out of that and hitched a jeep ride back to the Rustic area.

Bob Berry and Otto Walinski also returned that day. Otto was "inserted" into Katum just as it was overrun by the enemy. Otto spent the next three days escaping in one of the army's tanks.

They were trading stories at the Rustic bar when Maj. Bob Clifford told one that quieted the conversation a bit. The reason that they wanted single volunteers was that at least one and possibly two of them were not expected to return.

Back to Cambodia, in addition to providing air support for the activities on Routes 6 and 21, the Rustics were still flying cover over the large Mekong River convoys supplying Phnom Penh and the small boat convoys supplying Kompong Thom from the Tonle Sap. The Rustics found that using gunships to sterilize the area along the small convoys' route was very effective.

By October, the Cambodian army controlled a narrow strip of land that paralleled Route 6 from Skoun through Kompong Thma to Kompong Thom. Supply of Kompong Thom via the highway now became possible. In the third week of October, Lon Nol declared Chenla II to be a success, which it was not. Opening the road to Kompong Thom was a minor victory, but the Rustics suspected that it wouldn't last long. The distance from Skoun to Kompong Thom was about 70 miles (115 kilometers) and the Cambodian army had neither the strength nor the weapons to control that much territory. The U.S. Army faced a similar problem in South Vietnam, that of maintaining control of the Major highways. They did it by removing all vegetation for several hundred yards on either side of the highway and constantly patrolling it with assault helicopters. The Cambodian army could not do either.

Shortly after Lon Nol's declaration of success, NVA sappers blew up a bridge southwest of Skoun on Route 6, which made use of the highway impossible. It cut the link between the Cambodian Chenla forces and their supplies. During the next week, the NVA cut Route 6 in several places, which essentially isolated the Cambodian battalion garrisoned in the town of Rumlong.

Rumlong was a small town located about two thirds of the way between Skoun and Kompong Thma. The NVA Ninth Division surrounded Rumlong and began setting up mortars for an attack. They would sight the mortars on the town and then bury them so that only the tip of the mortar tube was visible. These were undetectable from the air and this technique gave the NVA plenty of time to organize their attack. At the time, the *Stars and Stripes* newspaper reported that sixty enemy bunkers were surrounding Rumlong. The source of that news was a mystery, but it was probably correct.

With the attacks along Route 6, the Rustics were suddenly back in the business of dealing with troops-in-contact situations. By now, the Rustics were operating out of Ubon and were starting to get replacement pilots who had been through French language school. In early November, Doug Aitken had one of them, Bob Andrews, in his backseat for an initial checkout.

They flew to Rumlong and put in air strikes supporting relief columns coming from both the north and the south. The army commander at Rumlong spoke neither English nor French and had to relay his situation and requests in Cambodian to the commander moving down from the north. The Rumlong commander requested air strikes right on the edge of his position, which Doug thought was much too close. Because of the lack of direct communication with the commander at Rumlong, Blue Chip disapproved that target, but did approve targets both north and south of the town in support of the relief forces. All of this was relayed from Blue Chip through Ramrod, the ABCCC plane orbiting the area at high altitude.

Doug and Bob planned to use the first set of fighters in support of the southern relief column, but when they showed up (Hawk 05 flight, A-37s from Bien Hoa), the commander of the northern column announced that he had a TIC and was taking mortar, 12.7mm and small arms fire. Ramrod approved the change of the fighters' targets.

The A-37s each carried four cans of napalm and two pods of HE rockets in addition to two thousand rounds of 7.62 mini-gun ammunition. Because napalm was delivered at a very low altitude (500 feet), the A-37s were vulnerable to ground fire and had developed a new tactic. Hawk Two orbited low out of sight of the target while Hawk Lead rolled in high and ripple-fired one pod of rockets on the target. Ripple-firing shot nineteen rockets sequentially and provided some dispersion of the rockets. Hawk Two timed his pass to be over the target immediately after the rockets hit and released two cans of napalm. After two of these passes they reversed roles. In effect, the rocket pass forced the enemy to keep their heads down while the other fighter made his low altitude napalm pass. This significantly reduced the number of hits taken by the fighters.

Now, Hawk Lead was out of rockets and Hawk Two was out of napalm and they were ready to switch positions. All of a sudden, the Rumlong commander came on the radio yelling something that neither Doug nor Bob could understand, but they could tell he was in a panic. The northern ground commander translated and told Doug that the NVA were coming over the perimeter and infiltrating the Rumlong commander's position. The northern commander relayed the target coordinates, which were the same ones Blue Chip had disapproved. Doug had no authority to hit that target.

"Thinking there might have been an error in transmitting the coordinates, I put in a mark (WP rocket) about 165 feet (50 meters) north of the coordinates he had given me. The northern commander relayed, 'Good smoke, but go south 20 meters. He is really getting hit hard!' "

Doug declared a tactical emergency, a procedure that allowed a FAC to provide immediate support to a ground commander in a TIC situation without waiting for clearance. He told the Hawk fighters to come down to Rumlong, and he made three or four passes using his own HE rockets. There were hooches built on stilts on either side of the highway north of town and Doug could see the enemy fire coming from under the hooches. He marked the location and cleared the fighters in. They did beautiful work with Hawk Lead dropping one can of napalm at a time and splashing it under the hooches. Suddenly, the northern commander relayed, "Good! Move 20 more meters south!"

The A-37s and Doug's OV-10 had nothing left but ammunition for their machine guns, so they moved 20 meters south and all three aircraft made strafing passes until their guns were empty. They watched each other closely and all three aircraft were being hosed (taking ground fire) on their passes.

Doug's replacement, Rustic 18 (Tom Clinch) was on station and monitoring the action. He had already ordered more air support through Ramrod and, after a quick briefing from Doug, was ready to take over the tactical emergency. Doug and the Hawk fighters were both low on fuel and had nothing left to shoot or drop, so they headed home.

OV-10 rolls in to mark a target, November 1971. Doug Aitken collection.

Tom Clinch continued the air support. About twenty minutes later, Ramrod came on the radio and said, "Rustic 16 and Rustic 18, put no more ordnance on those grids. I repeat: put no more ordnance on those grids!"

"Oh s——t," Doug thought, "There goes my career." Obviously Seventh Air Force did not appreciate FACs attacking targets they had previously disapproved. Just as Doug and Bob crossed the Thailand border, he heard Tom report that the NVA had abandoned their attack on Rumlong and everything was under control. Any official displeasure of the actions of the Rustics suddenly disappeared.

The Rustics continued to support the forces at Rumlong for two more weeks until it finally fell to the NVA on November 13. The battle had lasted for nineteen days. According to the *Stars and Stripes* newspaper, the Cambodian army had to leave more than four hundred wounded behind while three hundred survivors escaped the town at 1 A.M. In the end, the friendly perimeter at Rumlong was no larger than a football field and it was simply overrun by NVA troops. Rustic-controlled air strikes destroyed Rumlong and the equipment the Cambodians had left behind. Many years later, Doug Aitken discussed the destruction of Rumlong with Colonel Oum: "Rumlong was Oum's hometown and he is the one that ordered it destroyed. He knew that wounded soldiers had been abandoned there and if they hadn't been killed by the NVA, they were killed by our air strikes. As he told me this, his eyes were full of tears."

The NVA were not done. The next town north of Rumlong was Baray. The NVA cut the highway between Baray and Kompong Thma thus denying it any support from Kompong Thma and capturing it with the same tactics used at Rumlong.

Kompong Thma was next. The NVA tactics were simple and obvious. They would isolate a town by cutting the only highway in and out. This meant the garrison in the town could not be reinforced or resupplied. Then they would encircle the town and set up an attack preceded by mortar and artillery bombardment. They would usually leave a segment of the circle open so that the Cambodian soldiers could escape. When the Cambodians tried to use that route, the NVA would close it and have the Cambodian soldiers surrounded in the open and unprotected by the structures in the town. The Cambodian army units were not strong enough to mount an offensive attack against the NVA and they would merely wait for the attack they knew was coming. In effect, this ceded the decisions on whether, when, and where to attack to the NVA. The Cambodian's only defensive strategy was to ask the Rustics to provide air support after the attack started.

Air support was furnished, and it was effective, but not effective enough to defeat the attack. Close air support depends primarily on knowing exactly where the enemy is and exactly where to drop the munitions. This was essentially the job of the FAC in coordination with the ground commander. If the ground commander waited until he was attacked to identify the enemy positions, it was too late. The opportunity to destroy the enemy before he attacked or at least limit his ability to attack had already been lost. If the NVA soldiers could get close enough to the Cambodian positions so that bombs could not be used without endangering the friendly troops, the battle was won—or lost, depending on your point of view. Full air support could no longer be used effectively.

On December 1, 1971, Doug Aitken, Rustic 16, flew one of the final missions over Kompong Thma and described it as both the most exciting and disheartening mission of his tour. His backseater was Doug Norman, Rustic Mike.

They flew down from Ubon and entered a battle already in progress. Les Gibson, Rustic 01, with Marcel Morneau, Rustic Victor, had put in seven air strikes in support of Hotel 21 who was now the commander of the garrison at Kompong Thma. The situation was very bad. Hotel 21 had troops along Route 6 to the southwest and Route 21 to the southeast. Sam, his radio operator, reported, "Our troops are cut into three pieces, sir. We cannot join each other, sir." The main body of troops in the town was under constant mortar and artillery attack. Sam was beginning to lose his normally calm attitude.

"Send a message immediately to your headquarters, sir. Situation is very bad. (The Cambodian word for it is) *bacal*. Do you know *bacal*? One more word for you, sir. The end might be today, sir. My superior's car destroyed by a rocket. He is injured and the driver is killed. Do you know what 'Hari Kari' is? Some soldiers are doing the same thing."[5]

The fighters check in and Doug Norman was talking to Sam to pinpoint enemy locations. Hawk 03 flight was A-37s with Mk-82 bombs, rockets, and mini-guns. The plan was to use the fighters to unpin the troops along Route 21 so they could escape back to Kompong Thma. As Doug Aitken was about to begin the air strike, Sam called out four more grids and a new plan. These grids were north of the town across the river. Sam wanted them destroyed so that the friendly troops could escape to that area from Kompong Thma.

"Kompong Thma will be completely destroyed within five hours," according to Sam. The fighters destroyed the nearest grid with their bombs, but Hotel 21 refused to evacuate his troops until all four of the grids were destroyed. Doug Aitken ordered more airpower and took the Hawk fighters south to expend their rockets and guns in support of the friendly troops on Route 6. In the process, the Hawks got hosed by at least three 12.7mm gun sites in a small village west of Route 6.

"Destroy the village, sir. There are no friendly troops there. There are many many (enemy) guns coming up from the village." The Hawks expended all of their rockets and guns and wished Sam "good luck" as they headed for home. The A-37s were the only fighters with FM radios and thus they carried the only fighter pilots who could monitor the action and gain a real understanding of what was going on down there.

OV-10 on a low altitude rocket attack. U.S. Air Force collection.

This was obviously going to be a major air operation. Les Gibson, who was headed back to Ubon, called ahead to launch Bob Berry, Rustic 17, who was available to fly the backup aircraft. In addition, Phil Frischmuth, Rustic 55, came into the area. He had been escorting a Cambodian helicopter carrying "high officials."[6] He was monitoring the battle and could tell how busy Doug Aitken and Doug Norman were. He passed the current information through Ramrod to Blue Chip and ordered more air support.

When Bob Berry showed up, he and Doug Aitken developed a plan. Blue Chip would send the fighters to Bob on a different UHF frequency and he would brief them and turn them over to Doug on the UHF strike frequency. Doug would put them to work with no delay and no relief for the enemy between sets of fighters. The plan worked very well and the fighters destroyed the 12.7mm gun sites. Sam reported that the friendlies on Route 6 had moved back to Kompong Thma under cover of the air strikes.

Jerry McClellan, Rustic 14, checked in to relieve Doug Aitken, who was low on fuel and out of munitions. The excitement was over for Doug, but not for Sam and his commander, Hotel 21. Kompong Thma only lasted for one more day.

Ron Van Kirk, Rustic 08, with Marcel Morneau, Rustic Victor, in his backseat was there at the end. Kompong Thma had been overrun and an A-37 had been shot down earlier in the day. The pilot was recovered safely after a hard-fought SAR (search and rescue) effort north of town. The Cambodian forces were retreating north along Route 6 to Kompong Thom.

The weather was bad and getting worse. Hawk 05 flight had been scrambled from Bien Hoa. It was getting dark; it was raining and the ceiling was dropping. Ron's mission was to destroy the store of ammunition the Cambodians had left in Kompong Thma. The NVA was already in Kompong Thma and there was intense ground fire from both small arms and at least five separate 12.7mm antiaircraft gun emplacements.

Ron and the Hawk fighters modified the normal rules slightly. They hid in the clouds except for target run-ins. One of the fighters would call, "Out of the clouds, heading ————." Ron would pop out of the clouds, pick up the fighter, mark the target, clear him to hit it, and pop back into the clouds. The glow of the fires resulting from their attack gave them a reference point to help maintain their orbit while still in the clouds.

Hawk 06 went first with bombs to protect Hawk 05's napalm passes. Unfor-

Two Rustics, out of rockets, return to Ubon, November 1971. Doug Aitken collection.

tunately, Hawk 05 went through dry (no release of munitions) on two passes due to target identification problems. Hawk 06 was now out of bombs and Hawk 05's napalm passes suddenly became very dangerous. Ron rolled in with HE rockets followed by Hawk 06 with strafe to protect Hawk 05's napalm runs. That did the job and the ammunition cache abandoned in Kompong Thma exploded and burned brightly against the low clouds. Ron and the Hawk fighters headed for home with some satisfaction at having defeated the rotten weather and the intense enemy ground fire. In spite of that, it was still a bad day for the Cambodians at Kompong Thma.

On December 4, 1971, *Stars and Stripes* carried the following report.[7]

> The decision to abandon the town of Kompong Thma, which was evacuated Thursday (December 2, 1971), was taken against the wishes of the local commander, Col. Um Savuth, who wanted to hold the town. The evacuation was carried out in an orderly fashion despite several days of heavy fighting. Um Savuth was thus able to save most of his heavy equipment and trucks. With the loss of Rumlong, Baray, and Kompong Thma, the NVA now control virtually all of Highway 6 between Skoun and Tang Krasang.

On December 3, 1971, Operation Chenla II was officially terminated. It was, by any measurement, a victory for the NVA. *Newsweek* magazine of December 13, 1971 reported:

> The NVA offensive succeeded in (1) preventing the Lon Nol government from securing control of the record rice crop now being harvested along Route 6, and (2) protecting the communists' supply Routes into Laos at the start of the dry season.

That was an understatement.

10

Ubon, Thailand

In July 1971, Tom Adams's tour was up and Lt. Col. Walter Arellano took command of the Rustics.

At Bien Hoa, things were changing rapidly. The process of Vietnamization was accelerating and Bien Hoa was going to be returned to the Vietnamese. By mid-August, there was serious talk about cut backs and consolidation. Other units could cut back their mission and consolidate their operations, but politically, the Rustics were still committed to supporting Cambodia. There would be no cutback. Chenla II began in August and the Rustics were as busy as ever. Walt Arellano was given the task of developing a plan to move out of Bien Hoa and continue to provide full Cambodian support while doing so.

The closing of a base the size of Bien Hoa while there was still a war to be fought was chaotic. There were Vietnamese to be trained to fly the airplanes they would be given, critical supplies to be packed and shipped back as cargo, personnel to be transferred or (they hoped) sent back to the United States—it was a big mess. You checked your mailbox at the post office every day because there was no assurance the post office would be there tomorrow. It was obvious that the Rustics could not stay at Bien Hoa under any conditions. Shortly there would be no fuel, no munitions, no food, and no support.

An early plan was to move the Rustics to Tan Son Nhut in Saigon and let them operate from there. That was unacceptable for the same reasons the Rustics left Tan Son Nhut a year earlier. There was no room and no support for the aircraft. In September, it looked like the Rustic OV-10s would move to Ubon Royal Thai Air Force Base in Thailand.

Ubon was one of six air bases in Thailand used by the United States Air Force.[1] It had plenty of room and could support the Rustic OV-10 operation. It was located due North of Phnom Penh and the flying time from Ubon to Phnom Penh was roughly one third greater than it was from Bien Hoa. Considering the OV-10's endurance with the big belly tank, this still gave the Rustics about three and a half hours of useful time in the target area.

The question was what to do with the Rustic O-2s. There was talk of moving them to the Mekong delta region of South Vietnam and having them continue flying as Tilly or Sundog FACs. The Tilly and Sundog FACs had been assigned to the Nineteenth TASS Task Force (which included the Rustics), and they also came under Walt Arellano's command. They had been flying some of the Cambodian missions from the delta region for nearly a year. This was a span-of-control problem for Walt and he spent a lot of his time traveling among the three bases.

Fortunately, he had some very strong leaders at each location. Major Womack ran the Sundogs at Tan Son Nhut and Major Perret had the Tillys at Binh Thuy. At Bien Hoa, he had Major Clifford for the Rustic OV-10s and Major Roberds for the Rustic O-2s. All were experienced and knew what had to be done and how to do it.

There were several problems with moving the O-2s to Ubon. Under the U.S. Status of Forces Agreement[2] (SOFA) with Thailand, there was a limit to the number of U.S. personnel who could be stationed there. The agreement could accommodate most of the OV-10 operation, but the O-2 operation would put them well over the limit. Also, the added flight time from Ubon to central Cambodia significantly reduced the O-2's effective mission time.

The final decision was to move the OV-10 Rustics to Ubon. The Nineteenth TASS would move to Phan Rang Air Base and be combined with the Twenty-first TASS where they would set up an O-2 training program. The Rustic OV-10 pilots were assigned to the Twenty-first TASS for a short time until the Status of Forces Agreement with Thailand could be straightened out. Then, the Rustic OV-10 pilots were officially assigned to Ubon as FOL #1 of the Twenty-third TASS at Nakhon Phanom. The Rustic O-2 pilots were reassigned to the new TASS at Phan Rang, the Sundogs at Tan Son Nhut or the Tillys at Binh Thuy. The Night Rustic O-2 operation itself was deactivated.

The Night Rustics only existed for fourteen months, but that small group of pilots literally wrote the book on night FAC operations in direct support of ground commanders. Because the mission was highly classified and there were so few people involved, the Night Rustics never received the recognition they deserved. Flying at low altitude at night over a combat zone where there were no lights on the ground and no navigation aids took a special kind of bravery. Even if there was no enemy activity, that was an inherently dangerous way to operate an airplane. The Night Rustics earned the respect of everyone familiar with the Rustic operation.

As part of Vietnamization, Walt Arellano had been given a few other tasks that had nothing to do with the Rustics. He was frequently out of the country and Maj. Les Gibson became the Rustics' acting commander for the purpose of moving to Ubon. He became the official Rustic commander after they had arrived at Ubon.

One result of the move to Ubon was a reduction in the number of back-seaters. In addition to the limitations on personnel in Thailand, most of the original group of backseaters had served their tour and some were serving on voluntary tour extensions. The Rustics only took nine backseaters with them to Ubon. These were the newest ones who had the most time remaining on their tours. By the time their tour was up, the Rustics expected to be getting new OV-10 pilots who had completed French language school.[3]

Les Gibson had several meetings at Seventh Air Force and made two trips to Ubon to coordinate the move with the host unit, the Eighth Tactical Fighter Wing. He arranged for hooches, maintenance hangars, flight operations build-ings, and parking ramp space for the aircraft. Because the OV-10 cadre slightly exceeded the Thailand personnel limits, some personnel were techni-cally still assigned to the Twenty-first TASS at Phan Rang, but were on tem-porary duty (TDY) orders to Ubon. That was one way of circumventing the personnel limitation of the SOFA.

The Rustic pilots and backseaters moved the airplanes. They could fit all of their personal belongings in the cargo compartment, fly a mission over Cam-bodia and land at Ubon. For the rest of the move, Les Gibson used five C-130s to move all the support people and all the maintenance, supply, office, and in-telligence equipment. Some of the C-130s made more than one trip and the move was essentially completed in two days.

Missue, the Rustic mascot, was put in a box and loaded onto a C-130. She did not like that at all and ended up riding on the flight deck and making friends with the crew.

When the Rustics were designated as a Nineteenth TASS Task Force, they acquired their own chief of maintenance, Senior M. Sgt. Don Corrie. He turned out to be an essential element in the move.

Since Bien Hoa was closing, almost everything there was up for grabs, so to speak. Don Corrie loaded all the spare parts he could find for the OV-10s plus all the bunk beds, foot lockers, wall lockers, typewriters, lawnmowers, and

M-16 assault rifles that no one else seemed to want. The Rustics arrived at Ubon as one of the best equipped units on the base. Most of the M-16s were eventually given to the Cambodians; another illegal arms transaction that would have made Doc Thomas (Rustic X-Ray) proud.

At Ubon, the Rustics were officially designated as Operating Location #1 (OL-1) of the Twenty-third TASS at Nakhon Phanom RTAFB. Nakhon Phanom (also known as NKP or sometimes "Naked Fanny" or "Naked Phantom" in honor of their special forces operations) was on the Laotian border and about a forty-five-minute flight due north of Ubon. The Twenty-third TASS owned the Nail FACs whose mission was almost entirely in Laos over the Ho Chi Minh trail. The Rustics at Ubon were still under the direct control of Blue Chip at Seventh Air Force, so this really wasn't much of a change in their organizational structure. They were getting the same administrative support from the Twenty-third TASS that they had from the Nineteenth TASS at Bien Hoa.

The munitions load for the OV-10 at Ubon was slightly different. It carried the same 230-gallon fuel tank on the center station along with the four M-60 machine guns in the sponsons. On the outboard sponson stations, though, it carried LAU-3 rocket pods each loaded with nineteen HE rockets. The inboard stations carried LAU-59 pods with seven rockets each. One pod carried WP marking rockets while the other pod carried flechette rockets. After being fired, the case of these rockets opened deploying hundreds of small dart-like flechettes. This could be a devastating antipersonnel weapon. This load reduced the OV-10's target marking capability but increased its attack capability. This recognized the reduction of fighter availability due to the drawdown in Vietnam. Thus the Rustic mission shifted slightly toward attack and away from control of other fighters.

On the downside, this almost doubled the rocket load and the extra weight and drag made takeoff performance even more critical than it was at Bien Hoa. The takeoff performance was now literally "beyond the performance charts" in the OV-10 flight manual. The critical single engine failure speed (minimum control speed) was now above takeoff speed. This meant that an engine failure immediately after takeoff would result in an uncontrollable roll into the dead engine. To cope with this, the Rustic pilots held the plane on the ground until they achieved critical engine failure speed so that they could either fly the plane or eject from it if an engine quit. At Ubon, the OV-10s needed most of the runway to get airborne, which impressed even the F-4 fighter pilots. There was no margin for error. The slightest engine problem on takeoff meant that the pilot had to immediately jettision all rocket pods and

Rear view of an OV-10 at Ubon showing the weapons load used there. The machine guns are in the "sponsons" that support the rocket pods. Ron Van Kirk collection.

the fuel tank and retract the gear if the plane had achieved flying speed—or eject if it hadn't. There was no time to think about it. On each takeoff of that type, the plane reached a point where it cannot stop in the runway remaining, but it is not yet going fast enough to fly. Until the plane reached flying speed, the pilot is essentially just a passenger. If anything happens, he has no choice but to eject.

Since the Rustics were not located on the same base with their parent TASS, they had their own maintenance section headed by Don Corrie. The maintenance was superb. In January 1972, for example, 205 sorties were scheduled, but 215 were actually flown. That's almost seven sorties a day. There was only one mission abort and one late takeoff due to maintenance. Don Corrie continued building his reputation as the best "scrounge" in the Air Force. When he needed a UHF radio, for example, and was not getting any satisfaction from the base supply system, he had a last ditch scheme that worked several times.

Ubon was home to several AC-130 Spectre gunships, which each carried two UHF radios. Don would put on an AC-130 Spectre maintenance hat, drive up to an AC-130, and swap out his inoperable radio for a good one. He always meticulously entered this fact in the aircraft logbook so the AC-130 folks wouldn't be completely surprised. "What the hell," he reasoned, "they can fly with only one working UHF radio and their maintenance officer can probably shake a new one loose from the supply system easier than I can."

In January 1972, Lt. Col. Ray Stratton took over as Rustic Commander from Les Gibson. One of his first acts was to order Don Corrie to stop stealing radios from the Spectres. He watered that down considerably by flying Don back to Bien Hoa on two occasions for the specific purpose of scrounging needed aircraft parts from the Vietnamese Air Force. In a combat situation, one of the marks of a good commander is to know when the rules aren't working and not let that affect the unit's combat capability. It didn't.

Unlike the maintenance troops at Bien Hoa who belonged to the Nineteenth TASS, the Ubon maintainers were Rustics and identified with that organization. They invented a gag they would spring on new OV-10 pilots. It took advantage of the fact that new pilots had never flown with an external fuel tank and knew little about it. When empty, the tank was quite light and easy to remove. After the new pilot had landed from a mission and parked, it took over a minute for the propellers to stop spinning so he could get out of the airplane. In that one-minute period, the maintenance troops would remove the fuel tank

Ubon Royal Thai Air Force Base, Thailand. U.S. Air Force collection.

and hide it somewhere. When the pilot finally got out, one of the maintenance people would ask, "Captain, what happened to your centerline fuel tank?" The pilot, of course, didn't know and couldn't explain it. He had visions of being hauled up before his new commander to explain the loss of a valuable fuel tank. The maintenance guys would finally tell him what happened and that would keep them amused until the next new pilot showed up.

Living conditions at Ubon were better than they were at Bien Hoa. Even though Bien Hoa was a fully equipped air base, it was in a combat zone with actual fighting in the vicinity and the occasional rocket attack. Since Thailand wasn't directly involved in the conflict, life was relatively peaceful. Americans shopped and dined in the nearby villages and occasionally spent a night or two in Bangkok, which had excellent military recreation and shopping facilities. Pilots were authorized three days a month in Bangkok, which included golf, sightseeing, and whatever. Because of the distance, the trip to Bangkok required a night on the train each way, but it was worth it just to get a short vacation from combat. Compared to Saigon, it was almost a resort. Because Thailand was not a combat area, it was possible for an American dependent, usually a wife, to travel to Bangkok to join her husband. There were a number of military personnel assigned to three-year tours in Thailand and the American dependent population was quite large.

By October 1971, the Rustics were well established at Ubon. The move was made with no interruption in the support of the Cambodians and Chenla II continued into December with very heavy fighting.

11

No Rest for the Rustics

Although Chenla II had officially ended, nobody told the NVA. The fighting was still going on and the Rustics were still maintaining round-the-clock coverage over Cambodia. January was supposed to be in the middle of the dry season, but "wet" and "dry" were relative terms. The weather in Cambodia was highly unpredictable and there was no such thing as a daily weather briefing or forecast for Cambodia. The Rustics learned the weather by launching a plane on a mission and having the pilot radio the weather news back to Ubon. The OV-10 was fully instrumented and the Rustics were all qualified instrument pilots, so the weather was more of a nuisance than a serious problem. The worst part of it was trying to stay beneath the clouds and above the ground fire. An airplane silhouetted against cloud cover was an easier target for the enemy.

In January 1972, Ron Van Kirk, Rustic 08, was flying solo on his way south to Kompong Cham when the clouds closed down and he was in them whether he liked it or not. He climbed to 10,000 feet, which didn't help. He couldn't pick up a navigation signal from either Phnom Penh or Saigon and there was nobody on the ground who could help. They didn't know where he was either.

He turned north to head back to Ubon as there was nothing he could accomplish by flying around in the soup. After about fifteen minutes, he managed to fly into a thunderstorm and things got really nasty. There was severe turbulence, constant lightning, and torrential rain. Maintaining a precise altitude or heading was impossible. Just keeping the plane right side up and out of a stall took all his efforts. That lasted for over an hour. Eventually, he flew out of the storm and could climb into blue sky, but he still couldn't talk to anyone or pick up any navigation aid. He had been flying for nearly four hours and had no idea where he was.

His only option was to descend and pickup a landmark. He made a slow descent back into the clouds and finally broke out at about 1,000 feet over water. Nothing but water as far as he could see. It looked like he was over the ocean, but which ocean? He decided that continuing to fly north was still his best hope. If he couldn't find himself fairly quickly, fuel would become a problem.

He finally reached land, but it was flooded and he couldn't identify anything. He kept flying and eventually recognized the temples at Angkor north of Siem Reap. He had descended over the Tonle Sap (great lake), which was big enough to confuse anyone. It was still a forty-five-minute flight from Angkor to Ubon, and Ron spent it watching the fuel gage and thinking about what a really bad day it had been so far.

In February, Ron was flying another mission with Roger Hamann (Rustic Yankee) as his backseater. The weather was deteriorating, but wasn't bad yet. Ron headed for Kompong Thom and checked in with Shad Kimbell (Rustic 10), whom he was replacing. Shad had been working with Sam (Hotel 21 had retreated back to Kompong Thom after the fall of Kompong Thma) and already had a target approved and Hawk 05 flight (A-37s) on the way for Ron to use. With Ron in sight, Shad marked the targets for him and headed home as he was low on fuel. On his way out, he advised that they had confirmed 12.7mm AA guns in the area. Ron contacted Sam and got a quick update on friendly troop movements as Hawk 05 checked in.

Ron went through the standard briefing litany: known enemy location, tree covered area, tops to 90 feet, weather 4,500 feet scattered, visibility 10 miles in haze, strong winds on the surface estimated 20–25 knots from the south, friendlies one klick southwest of the target in a pagoda, expect ground fire from 12.7mm AA, bail-out area is the town of Kompong Thom, alternate recovery Phnom Penh heading 185 degrees, 70 nautical miles, random run-in headings approved, FAC holding at 4,000 feet, plan two passes each.

"Roger. Hawk 05 copies. We're descending through 7,000 feet, give us some smoke." Ron gave them a two-second burst of smoke from his smoke tank.

"FAC's in sight. Ready for your mark." Ron rolled in to mark the target with a WP rocket.

"Hawk lead's in from the northwest, I have your mark."

"I have you in sight, lead, cleared hot."

"Lead's off."

"Good bomb, lead. Two, drop about 15 meters short of Lead's bomb."

"Roger. Two's in."

"Cleared hot."

"Nice secondary explosion! Lead, go about 5 meters beyond two's bomb."

"Lead's in."

"Cleared hot."

"Another nice secondary explosion. We've got something here."

"Rustic 08, this is Sam. The ground commander is reporting that the fighters are taking heavy ground fire from just north of the target area."

"Roger that, Sam, I see it too."

"Rustic, Hawk lead. I saw tracers from that area on my last pass, too." (A-37s had FM radios and could monitor the ground conversation.)

"OK guys, lets move the next run about 25 meters north and get the guns. Rustic's in to mark. Hit my smoke."

"Two's in from the west."

"In sight. Cleared hot. Shack! Real nice! Lead, put your bomb 10 meters short of that last one, and Two, you go ten meters long." (Two more perfect hits by the Hawks resulted in a large secondary explosion).

"Rustic 08, this is Sam. The ground commander reports that the bombs have blown many guns into the air."

"Roger that, Sam."

"Rustic, this is Hawk lead. You were taking ground fire just south of your smoke."

"Roger, Hawk, let's try the mini-guns on that position. Do you need another mark?"

"Negative, Lead's in."

"Cleared hot."

"Two's in."

"Cleared hot."

"That's pretty heavy fire, Rustic, looks like it might be a 12.7 quad."

"Roger, let's knock it off. We can't deal with that with just our mini-guns. We'll get it next time with bombs."

Ron thanked the Hawks for a superb job and gave them their BDA; three large secondary explosions and one gun emplacement destroyed. Ron cleared them to RTB.

Ron checked in again with Sam. Hotel 303 (Colonel Oum) had just landed after returning from Phnom Penh. He came on the radio.

"I just got off the plane and wanted to let you know that we have no firm date yet for our trip to Ubon. Things need to get a bit quieter before we can come. It looks like the last week of February is out, maybe sometime in March."

"No problem. We will be ready whenever you can make it." Oum had a standing invitation to visit the Rustics at Ubon as he had at Bien Hoa and to bring Sam with him.

Ron arranged for a gunship to provide overnight protection at Kompong Thom and headed back to Ubon. For the Rustics, it had been just another normal day at the office.

About this time, President Nixon made his historic visit to China. Some sort of peace negotiations were in the works. The results of the drawdown of U.S. Forces in South Vietnam were becoming obvious. The remaining fighters and FACs could barely keep up with the workload. The Rustics were still the largest single group of experienced FACs in South East Asia and some of them were sent temporarily to NKP to help the Nail FACs with their missions in the Steel Tiger area of southern Laos.[1]

When the Rustics were still at Bien Hoa, the Sundog and Tilly FACs had been assigned to the Nineteenth TASS Task Force. They flew O-2s and in March 1972 they were still actively flying Rustic-type missions from Tan Son Nhut and Binh Thuy. Normally, they would cover the southern portion of Cambodia, but occasionally they would get as far north as Phnom Penh.

Doug Aitken, Rustic 16, was in the vicinity of Kompong Thom with Joe Garand, Rustic Echo, in the backseat. Doug was working with Hawk A-37s when he got a call on VHF from Sundog Alpha (the radio relay station on Nui Ba Den) asking if he could bring his fighters down to Phnom Penh. Sundog Alpha had heard a Mayday call on the radio. He suspected it was from Sundog 12, who was operating southwest of Phnom Penh. Doug broke off his activity at KPT and gave the Hawks a new rendezvous point near Phnom Penh. Because of their speed, they arrived well ahead of Doug. They had no VHF radios, but they did have FM and they attempted to contact Sundog 12 on all tactical frequencies.

Sundog Alpha had initiated the search and rescue (SAR) system and Doug was designated as the "on-scene commander." In addition, he had Ray Stratton, Rustic 03, who had just entered Cambodia from Ubon and was following Doug to Phnom Penh. Hawk lead reported that they had contact with someone on UHF 243.0, the emergency frequency preset into all survival radios. There was a pretty good chance that Sundog 12 was down, but alive.

Since the location was not known, Doug and Ray set up a weaving search pattern starting at the last known target coordinates. The survivor, who was apparently the interpreter; not the pilot, told the Hawk fighters that he was staying close to his parachute so he could be identified, but he could not see any landmarks that would help the Rustics locate him.

About fifteen minutes later, the survivor reported that he could hear engines. Doug and Ray alternatively "jazzed" their engines which gave the OV-10 a distinctive buzzing sound. The survivor reported that he couldn't hear either of them. Finally, Doug and Ray got close enough to hear the survivor on UHF. That helped, because the OV-10s carried UHF direction-finding equipment for just this purpose. Unfortunately, Ray Stratton's wasn't working and Doug wasn't yet close enough to get a good fix. Doug was using his UHF to provide a carrier tone for rescue helicopters to home in on him.

Doug was getting short of fuel and he was really pushing it. He could never make it back to Ubon, but he knew he could get fuel at Phnom Penh in an emergency. Doug was in a left bank when a U.S. Army rescue helicopter flew directly beneath him. The survivor yelled, "I see the helicopter. It's right over me!" Doug switched to FM, contacted the helicopter, and told him to go into orbit. He was very close to the survivor. Doug turned over command of the SAR to Ray and headed for Phnom Penh. The helicopter located the survivor and picked up the interpreter, S. Sgt. William Silva.

Sergeant Silva reported that his pilot, Lt. William Christie, Sundog 12, had been in orbit over the target when the enemy opened up with heavy AA fire. Lieutenant Christie was killed immediately. Sergeant Silva, who had only been in Vietnam a short time, grabbed the controls as he made the Mayday call heard by Sundog Alpha. When the front engine caught fire, he bailed out.

Doug made it to Phnom Penh and got his fuel. He remarked later that he didn't really need to look at the fuel gauge. All he had to do was ask his backseater what it said. In his rearview mirror he could see his backseater leaning far to the right with his eyes transfixed on the fuel gauge on the pilot's instrument panel.

The Rustics, Tillys, and Sundogs were never stationed together and didn't know each other personally. That didn't make any difference. When someone went down, the war came to a halt and all available aircraft headed for the scene to help in the SAR effort. If there were any Cambodian army units nearby, they came too. The knowledge that this would happen took some of the apprehension out of operating several hundred miles from friendly territory.

Colonel Oum made good on his promise to visit the Rustics at Ubon and bring Sam with him. In March, they flew by helicopter to Phnom Penh where they were picked up by two OV-10s and flown to Ubon. None of the Rustics at Ubon had ever met Sam face-to-face although they had all talked with him. Only the "old heads" who had been at Bien Hoa had ever met Oum.

Oum's visit to Ubon was very productive. They discussed tactics, both theirs and the enemy's, and established a Cambodian FAC training school at Ubon, similar to the one they had at Bien Hoa. Oum laid the groundwork for several Rustics to tour Cambodia in the coming months and visit the ground commanders they had been working with for so long. In late July, Ray Stratton, Jerry McClellan, Jack Thompson, and Marcel Morneau spent five days visiting major military installations in Cambodia. They met many of the ground commanders and discussed mutual capabilities and limitations in order to improve Rustic effectiveness.

Meanwhile, the war in South Vietnam was heating up. No one knew how the peace process would come out, but the North Vietnamese felt that if there was a truce, the lines would most likely be drawn at the positions that existed at that time. In their view, they should capture and hold as much of South Vietnam's territory as they could. If a truce was declared, they could expect to keep that territory. In early April, some of the Rustics were deployed to Tan Son Nhut for two weeks to fly missions in the Mekong delta region where there was intense fighting. This was also the start of the NVA Eastertide Offensive. The NVA pulled some of their units out of Cambodia and launched a heavy three-pronged attack against the South Vietnamese towns of Quang Tri, Kontum, and An Loc. Since the NVA action in Cambodia was reduced, many of the Rustics were deployed to Da Nang to help thwart the NVA offensive.

The deployment came about very quickly. The Rustics flew their planes to Da Nang at night and joined several Nail FACs who had been sent from NKP. The next day, they were flying combat missions together. Da Nang was a large air base on the seacoast in I Corps, about 105 miles (170 kilometers) south of the DMZ separating North and South Vietnam. Quang Tri was about 80 miles (130 kilometers) north of Da Nang on Route 1 near the DMZ. Kontum was 112 miles (180 kilometers) south of Da Nang. An Loc was 62 miles (100 kilometers) north of Saigon and not within range of Da Nang FACs. The Rustics were needed at Quang Tri and Kontum. This deployment was to last for two months.

On May 1, Quang Tri was abandoned to the enemy and South Vietnam's

Third ARVN division had, for all practical purposes, ceased to exist. South Vietnam's President, Nguyen Van Theiu, fired his senior commander in that area and replaced him with his best general, Ngo Quang Troung. When the Rustics arrived, the South Vietnamese forces had already retreated from Quang Tri and had abandoned hundreds of trucks, jeeps, and guns along the coastal highway (Route 1) south of Quang Tri. Many sorties were flown to destroy or disable the abandoned vehicles to prevent their capture. Regardless of the support from the VNAF and the U.S. Air Force, Quang Tri stayed in North Vietnamese hands.

This deployment showed the Rustics a new set of communist weapons. Because of the difficulty of transporting large weapons to Cambodia, the NVA units there were limited to small arms, mortars, and heavy machine guns, primarily the 12.7mm gun. The AA version of the 12.7mm was a deadly weapon against low flying aircraft and the Kalishnikov AK-47 assault rifle was superior to most of the weapons available to the Cambodian army.

At Quang Tri, the NVA used tanks and trucks that could bring artillery, rockets, and SA-7 Strela heat-seeking missiles. The Rustics didn't realize the SA-7 had a guidance system until they were shot down by one.

On May 25, Lt. Jim Twaddell, Rustic 24, was giving Lt. Jack Shaw, Nail 77, an orientation flight over the area near the DMZ. They were working a TIC with a U.S. Army unit that was pinned down by several NVA tanks. They could easily see the tanks, but could not accurately determine the friendly position. Suddenly Jack, who was flying the plane, saw a missile coming up. He thought it was an unguided B-40 missile until it made some hard turns toward the aircraft. It was a Strela heat-seeker and he knew they were in trouble.

The missile hit the OV-10's cargo compartment and started a fire just aft of the rear seat; probably in the hydraulic system. Don Brooks was shot down in a similar situation a year and a half earlier. Jack ejected just south of the DMZ and about 10 miles inland. Jim stayed with the plane and tried to make it offshore to the ocean. This was called "feet wet" and was considered the safest place to eject. The FACs wore life vests and carried a life raft in their survival kit and there were no enemy patrols in the ocean. The fire became too intense, though, and he ejected before reaching the coast. He landed among some sand dunes on the beach and was uninjured. Jack had landed in a rice paddy west of Route 1 and was likewise uninjured. Both were picked up within thirty minutes by ARVN helicopters and returned to Da Nang that evening.

The SA-7 Strela was a new weapon and no one knew much about it. Ray Stratton, the Rustic commander, reported what he knew to Seventh Air Force in Saigon and he was getting the idiot treatment from the Intell people down there. "There are no SA-7s. The NVA does not have SA-7s. Your plane was not shot down by an SA-7."

"About that time, I was having coffee with Lt. Col. Abe Kardong, the Covey FAC commander at Da Nang. He got a call from the security police at the main gate saying somebody wanted to talk to us about something. We jumped in Abe's jeep and drove down to the guard shack. There we found a Vietnamese civilian standing there holding two rocket tubes. They didn't look like anything I had ever seen, so I opened one up and I'm looking straight at the heat-seeker head of an SA-7. I asked the Vietnamese military policeman what the civilian wanted for them. He said, 'two packs of cigarettes.' He got two cartons of cigarettes and we got two brand new SA-7 Strelas. My phone call, a few minutes later, to Seventh Air Force in Saigon gave me an immense amount of satisfaction."

The Rustics also got into naval artillery bombardment. The FAC business actually got started back in World War II as a means of adjusting artillery fire. All FACs were trained to adjust artillery, but they seldom did it. Adjusting the bombardment from naval guns on ships off the coast was a little different, at least the lingo was different, and the Rustics usually carried a U.S. Marine warrant officer with them to handle the details. Chief Warrant Officer Wood was an expert on this and was flying with Ray Stratton, Rustic 03, one day.

"We had six tanks spotted, but we couldn't get any air support. Mr. Wood calmly came on interphone from the backseat and said, 'We'll handle that.' He contacted one of the Navy ships off shore—I don't know which one, it might have been the *New Jersey*—and directed the fire of their big guns. They destroyed all of the tanks in short order."

The NVA had brought a lot of Russian tanks across the DMZ and the Rustics got very proficient at spotting them and knocking them out with air strikes. They got so good that Seventh Air Force was beginning to question their BDA numbers and implied that Lieutenant Colonel Stratton was fudging the figures.

"On one occasion, General Slay [Gen. Alton Slay, Commander, Seventh Air Force] called me at Da Nang and demanded proof of our claimed tank kills. I asked for USAF recce [reconnaissance] photographs, but there weren't any. I was wondering what I was going to do when our favorite marine, Chief Warrant Officer Wood wandered into my office and asked what the problem was. I explained it to him and told him that without photographs, we couldn't prove that the Rustics and the Nails had killed the tanks we knew we had."

"Not a problem," Wood said, "I'll take care of it." He called out to the navy aircraft carrier operating off the coast and talked to the operations officer. The next day, the Navy flew a plane to Da Nang and delivered eight days worth of beautiful black-and-white pictures of destroyed tanks taken by their Vigilante reconnaissance squadron. The Rustics and Nails had claimed twenty-eight tanks destroyed, but there were actually thirty-two!

Ray Stratton called General Slay, who was slightly stunned by this news. He knew there were no USAF photographs, but it never occurred to him that the Navy was also flying recce missions and keeping close track of the battles. Les Gibson, Rustic 01, and Chief Warrant Officer Wood flew an OV-10 to Tan Son Nhut to personally deliver the photographs to General Slay and brief him on the missions. From then on, General Slay couldn't say enough good things about the Rustics. At the time, there was an ongoing attempt by the Commander of the Fifty-sixth Special Operations Wing at Nakhon Phanom (the host wing for the Twenty-third TASS) to break up the Rustics and distribute their assets to other FAC units. The Rustic's record of tank kills at Da Nang and General Slay's support put an end to that debate.

After the deployment, Ray Stratton went to Tan Son Nhut to brief General Slay and described the Rustics as being the general's "Swing FAC Squadron."

"I meant that the Rustics were fully qualified to work in Vietnam, Laos, or Cambodia and current on all three sets of Rules of Engagement. General Slay nodded his head and I heard later that he used the same expression when briefing COMUSMACV."

Down in the Kontum area, the NVA were using the same tactics they had used at Quang Tri. By May 4, Kontum was surrounded and virtually defenseless. The ARVN leadership at Kontum was no better than it had been at Quang Tri. President Thieu fired his senior commander in that area and replaced him with another excellent general, Nguyen Van Toan. The Rustics were flying many night missions and because of the distances involved, Ray Stratton set up a system where two pilots would fly an evening mission and recover to Pleiku, an air base about 22 miles (35 kilometers) south of Kontum to refuel and rearm. There, they would switch seats and fly a night mission, landing back at Da Nang in the early hours of the morning. These "Pleiku turns" as they were called, gave the FACs more hours over the target area with the same number of airplanes and pilots.

The OV-10 was not a good plane for night combat because of the way the canopy would pick up and magnify reflections of the plane's own instrument lights. Kontum was in the Vietnamese highlands and marking targets on a dark night was very difficult. The pilots would watch each other and the instruments for any signs of disorientation or vertigo. The target marking technique involved flares and log markers and was similar to the one used by the Rustic O-2s. The O-2s were better at it, though, because they could see better. In the OV-10, it was always a struggle to give the fighters a mark they could see before the flare burned out.

Jon Safley, Rustic 19, was flying one of these Pleiku turns with "H." Ownby, a Nail FAC in the backseat. The night was pitch black and they were working a TIC with an ARVN commander who didn't speak English. He was relaying his instructions through a U.S.Army advisor in Pleiku. That was always a high risk situation and the chances for error were multiplied. Jon completed the air strike, sent the fighters home, and called the Army advisor for BDA.

"I can't raise the ARVN commander. I think you may have had a short round." That was the one thing that no FAC wanted to hear. "Short round" was the code for munitions dropped on friendly troops.[2] All FACs have had the experience of watching a bomb or a can of napalm go slightly astray and had the terrible feeling that they might just have killed or wounded some of the people they were trying to protect. There is no feeling quite like it.

After about ten minutes, the Army advisor came back on the radio. "All is well. The bombs were close and frightened the ARVN troops. They dropped their radio as they ran and just now found it. No injuries."

Jon and "H." headed for Da Nang. They'd had enough excitement for one night.

President Nixon's reaction to the full-scale invasion from North Vietnam was to increase American airpower without increasing American ground forces. The increase included 119 more B-52s, four more Navy aircraft carriers and four Marine fighter squadrons. Nixon also launched Operation Linebacker, which included air strikes in North Vietnam and the mining of Haiphong Harbor.[3]

In the end, the ARVN counteroffensive headed by General Truong retook Quang Tri city and routed the six opposing NVA divisions. He did it with massive U.S. firepower including B-52s and offshore naval bombardment. In the Kontum area, General Toan had essentially the same success.

In the meantime, the fighting was still going on in Cambodia. The Rustics, even with the Tillys and the Sundogs helping, were spread very thin and the air support suffered. In May 1972, the American Embassy Air Attaché in Phnom Penh (Lt. Col. Mark Berent) complained about the lack of air support for the Cambodian army. With the ARVN counteroffensive going fairly well in Vietnam, the Rustics were sent back to Ubon and the war in Cambodia.

The problem in Cambodia was that there were few fighters available and the OV-10 could not carry a really effective load of weapons. In theory, it could carry five Mk-82 500 pound bombs, but that was without the external fuel tank and any marking rockets. At that weight, the OV-10 takeoff roll on a hot day at Ubon would attract spectators and bets might be placed.

There were Cambodian T-28s available, but Lt. Col. Kohn Oum was not there to lead them. He was still in the United States in advanced training courses, and most of the other Cambodian pilots did not speak English and lacked his experience.

After returning to Ubon, Jon Safley was working a target just east of Angkor. The rules of engagement were absolutely clear on the temples at Angkor: Do not put any munitions anywhere near them. Jon VR'd around the area and found piles of enemy supplies and some enemy spider holes (similar to the foxholes of WW II) plainly visible about 110 yards (100 meters) east of a wall around one of the smaller temples. He reported this to Blue Chip and went back to VR'ing. He didn't really expect an answer.

He was surprised when Blue Chip sent him a pair of Cambodian T-28s carrying Mk-82 slicks. That in itself was a slight violation of the rules of engagement. Rustic FACs weren't supposed to control Cambodian fighters (although they regularly did) and the FACs were definitely not to participate in anything that might result in damage to any pagoda, temple, monument, historical structure, or anything that looked like one. Someone was on duty at Blue Chip that day who clearly understood the situation and applied the best available solution to it.

Since the NVA spider holes paralleled the wall, it should be reasonably safe to run the fighters parallel to the wall. Bomb aiming errors were almost always in range, not azimuth. Jon briefed the fighters carefully and demonstrated the run-in heading he wanted as he marked the target.

"Got it?"

"Roger. Got it." The fighters then proceeded to run directly at the wall which was perpendicular to the briefed run-in line.

"Knock it off! Go through dry!" The fighters understood that and pulled off without dropping anything.

"OK. We'll be a three-ship flight and I'll be the leader. You follow me. OK?"

"OK."

Jon got the fighters in line to follow him. He rolled in and marked the target and pulled up into a standard fighter pattern to get ready for the next pass. Jon made four passes, firing a smoke rocket on each one, and the Cambodian fighter pilots hit his smoke every time. They had excellent BDA and the ground commander was very happy. The NVA was out of business in that area. There was nothing wrong with the skills of the Cambodian pilots. It was just their English that needed work.

In spite of all the training, no one really knows how they will react to a combat situation until they get involved in one. Ron Van Kirk was working a pair of F-4s from Ubon on a target just south of the Thai border. All three aircraft had been taking ground fire on every pass. The lead fighter had just pulled off and Ron was ready to clear the wingman in, but he couldn't find him and he didn't answer any radio calls. Ron and the lead fighter tried all frequencies, listened for an emergency signal on "guard" channel, and looked for any evidence of smoke that would indicate a crash. Lead climbed to a higher altitude and contacted Ubon Approach Control. The missing F-4 had just called in for landing instructions. Ron had two more hours to fly on his mission and spent much of it wondering what had happened to the F-4 wingman.

It was close to 8 P.M. when Ron landed, finished debriefing, and headed for the Officers Club for dinner.

> I found the intrepid aviator in the bar of the club and he was working on a good drunk. On the stool next to him was his flight helmet. You could clearly see where a 12.7mm round had gone in the front of his helmet and out the top. If you looked closely, you could see a matching mark where it had grazed his forehead on the way through. He had missed death by a mere fraction of an inch. When that happened, he just lit the afterburners and headed for home. He could remember nothing from the time he took the hit until he contacted Ubon for landing. This didn't seem like the right time to mention that a simple "good-bye" would have been appropriate, so I bought him another drink and headed for the dining room for dinner. It tasted unusually good.

August 1972 saw another Rustic milestone. The Rustic backseaters were being gradually replaced by newly arriving French-speaking OV-10 pilots. The final flights of the enlisted backseaters occurred on August 25. Roger Hamman (Rustic Yankee) flew with Jerry McClellan (Rustic 14) and Nick Lewis (Rustic Bravo) flew with Bob Andrews (Rustic 07.) Although they flew different missions, they returned to Ubon at the same time. Jerry and Bob joined in formation for the landing and taxied to the parking ramp together.

Nick and Roger were expecting the traditional champagne shower that came with the final combat flight. Roger got his, but Nick was doused with milk in deference to his Mormon religion. Thus ended a unique part of USAF history. For more than two years, nearly fifty enlisted men flew combat missions in a high performance tactical aircraft and became part of a unique combat team. They shared three characteristics. They were all volunteers; they were all dedicated to the mission; and, of course, they all spoke French. Without them, the Rustic story would have been a very short one.

In September 1972, Colonel Oum's disagreements with the military headquarters staff in Phnom Penh were beginning to catch up with him. The headquarters wanted to send his entire brigade to South Vietnam for training on the AR-15 assault rifle now being supplied by the Americans. Oum felt this was a waste of time and money. With ten or fifteen qualified AR-15 instructors, he could train his own brigade in just a few days right where they were. The entire brigade was sent to South Vietnam for training and when they returned, Colonel Oum was no longer their commander. He was reassigned as chief of staff of an army group at Siem Reap.

At Siem Reap, Oum found even more problems, particularly corruption, which was becoming widespread in the Cambodian army. Supplies meant for the army units continued to show up on the black market and in enemy hands. Nonexistent soldiers were filling the ranks while the real soldiers went unpaid and unfed. Greedy officers were buying Mercedes for themselves and jewelry for their wives.[4]

Oum refused to go along with any of this, so he was put in charge of a group of sixty officers sent to Political Warfare College in Taiwan.

Meanwhile, Phnom Penh was facing an acute shortage of rice in spite of all efforts to supply it by ship convoy. For the first time, transport aircraft were used to deliver rice to Phnom Penh. The city itself had been largely immune to the fighting, but was beginning to feel the impact of it.

In October, the Rustics were sent back to Tan Son Nhut to help the South Vietnamese army capture and hold portions of the southern delta region. The peace negotiations in Paris had changed from a cease-fire and withdrawal to prewar positions to a cease-fire in place.[5] The war was turning into a real estate grab. The Rustics worked with whatever fighters were available including Air Force, Navy, Marine Corps and VNAF. The A-7 "Sluf" (short little ugly fellow) had been in Vietnam since 1970 and used occasionally by the Rustics. Now, they were arriving in quantities to replace the A-1s as helicopter escorts on SAR missions and proved to be an excellent close air support fighter. It had good "play" time, carried a lot of munitions, and could deliver them very accurately. It also had a complete set of radios including FM.

While the Rustics were deployed to Tan Son Nhut, Lt. Col. Bill Ernst replaced Ray Stratton as Rustic commander. The Rustics flew 450 sorties from Tan Son Nhut before returning to Ubon in mid-December.

Back at Ubon, the Rustics began flying regular missions over the trail in the Steel Tiger area of Laos. That was a long flight from Ubon, but there was a lot of action. While they were still miles away, the Rustic pilots could see dust trails kicked up by the "movers" (North Vietnamese trucks carrying supplies down the Ho Chi Minh trail). The Rustics would use any available fighters or gunships. By now, the new C-130E Spectre gunships were equipped with both 20mm and 40mm guns and a 105mm howitzer. Watching one of those at work was an awesome sight.

Communications were a problem particularly if there were friendly Laotian army units in the area. In one case, Bill Ernst (Rustic 04) used an Air America plane that was carrying a Laotian passenger. The commander on the ground spoke to the passenger in Lao, who translated it in French to the Air America pilot, who relayed it to Bill Ernst in English, who could switch radios and instruct the fighters.

In late December, the Paris peace negotiations broke down and President Nixon sent B-52s to bomb Hanoi in an operation called Linebacker II. That restarted the peace negotiations and in early January, a treaty was signed calling for a cease-fire in Vietnam on January 29, 1973. The cease-fire in Laos would begin on February 23, 1973. There would be no cease-fire in Cambodia as Cambodia was not represented in Paris and was not part of the peace negotiation process.

On January 24, 1973, President Nixon announced the cease-fire in a speech to the American public. This led to an interesting situation halfway around the world in Cambodia.

Nixon's speech was picked up by Radio Australia and rebroadcast on their HF frequency. At the time, Rick Scaling (Rustic 09) was working with Sam (Hotel 21) and putting in an air strike near Prey Totung. He was talking to Sam on FM, and the fighters on UHF, which was all recorded on an ABCCC aircraft orbiting overhead. The ABCCC crew was also listening to Radio Australia on HF and portions of Nixon's speech were recorded in the background. Because the three radio frequencies were in use at the same time, portions of the tape were unintelligible. The intelligible parts contrast President Nixon's words with the words of an actual combat air strike in progress.[6]

Air Strike	President Nixon
R09: OK Lead. We'll want your CBU (cluster bomb units) just about another river's width to the north. The bad guys are running to the north and west out of that area, from that wooded section that's almost obscured by the smoke. Put it north of that.	
Lead: How far north?	
R09: About a river's width.	
Lead: OK.	
Sam: Zero Nine, sir, you are taking ground fire from where the CBU went off.	
R09: OK, and there's also ground fire from the areas of the CBU. Two, take time to set up.	. . . we shall also expect other interested nations to help ensure that the agreement is carried out . . .
R09: And the bad guys over in that area are still angry there.	
Lead: Haven't they heard the [cease-fire] news?	. . . as this long and difficult war ends . . .
R09: I don't think so. The friendlies in town have.	. . . your courage, by your sacrifice, you have won the precious right to determine your own future . . .
Two: Some people just can't take a joke.	
R09: Hah!	
R09: I hate to tell you this right now, but at this moment his speech is on Radio Australia. [R09 was also monitoring Radio Australia on HF]	. . . friends in peace as we have been allies in war.
Sam: Zero Nine, the bad guys are shooting at you from the dried up lake bed.	. . . let us now build a piece of reconciliation. For our part, we are prepared to make a major effort to help achieve that goal . . . so too will it be needed to build and strengthen the peace.
R09: Roger, Sam, I'll track them.	
Sam: Zero Nine you are taking ground fire, sir, from west of the target area again.	
R09: Roger.	. . . even indirectly, now is the time for mutual restraint . . .
R09: Cleared hot, Two, and there is ground fire from west of the target area.	. . . to all of you who are listening, the American people, your steadfastness . . .

R09: Roger, Two. Beautiful!

R09: There's a lot of irony today, gentlemen. Lead, I'll take your bombs in the wooded area. Let's put it in the wooded area just to the north of where Two's CBUs are in. You'll see the diamond-shaped pond and the first wooded area to the north of the diamond.

Sam: Zero Nine, requesting further CBUs.

Lead: OK, the wooded area with the heavy ground fire. Is it the same wooded area you're talking about?

R09: Negative, sir, the next wooded area to the northwest and it's in the northwest side of the CBU pattern.

Lead: OK, and you want to hit the wooded area?

R09: That's Charlie, sir. [That's correct, sir]

Lead: Just to the east, repeat, that wooded area just to the east of that pond.

R09: Roger that. Inside almost to the north of that diamond-shaped pond. It's on the west side of the CBU pattern. Just a hair to the east.

R09: OK, I'll get over there and put in a smoke. FAC's in with smoke in about twenty seconds.

R09: And Two, I'll be in with your smoke shortly.

R09: OK, Two, do you see my smoke? It's halfway between that diamond pond and the wooded area with the structure in it. I want you to hit that wooded area that's just to the northeast of my smoke.

Two: Two has the smoke.

. . . peace with honor possible.

. . . secret negotiations at the sensitive stage . . .

. . . those efforts. The important thing was not to talk about peace, but to get peace . . .

. . . achieved an honorable agreement, let us be proud . . .

. . . for the fifty million people of Indo-china. Let us be proud of the two and a half million young Americans . . .

. . . Let us be proud of those who gave their lives so that the people of South Vietnam might live in freedom and so that the world might live in peace. In particular, I would like to say a word to some of the bravest people I have ever met; the wives, children and families of our prisoners of war . . .

. . . so that where this generation knew war . . .

. . . next generation would know peace.

. . . yesterday, a great American who once occupied the office died. In his

R09: OK, sir, it's the wooded area that's just to the northeast of my smoke about two and a half river widths and it's north of that diamond.

Lead: I can't see the structure. Where is it? Which corner?

R09: It's almost dead center on the north side of it.

Sam: You are taking very heavy ground fire, sir, northwest of the target one klick.

R09: Lead, Sam reports very heavy ground fire northwest of the target one klick.

Lead: Got it.

R09: And it's close up to that pagoda. That's the reason we can't get near it.

Two: Roger.

R09: Roger, sir, Lead's cleared hot.

R09: Beautiful! OK, Two, I'll want yours to the right about a river's width from Lead's bomb.

Sam: Marvelous! Good pass! Right on, Right on!

Sam: Hit again! Hit again!

R09: Two, go ahead and hit that same area. Ground commander wants that same area hit. Cleared hot.

R09: Beautiful, Two. Lead, hit about a river's width north of Two's bombs. Cleared Hot.

life, President Johnson . . .

. . . nothing he cared about more deeply than achieving a lasting peace in the world.

. . . just the day after New Year's . . .

. . . concern with bringing peace, with making it the right kind of peace and I was grateful that he once again expressed his support . . .

No one would have welcomed this peace more than he.

Let us consecrate . . .

. . . thank you and good evening.

[Announcer, Radio Australia] That was Richard Nixon from Washington three hours ago, announcing that terms had been agreed to for peace in Vietnam.

And now we return to our regular program with Sonata Number . . .

[Symphonic music]

After the cease-fire in Vietnam on January 29, the Rustic activity in Laos picked up. The North Vietnamese were still rushing supplies down the Ho Chi Minh trail to their units in South Vietnam. Fighters that could no longer be used in Vietnam found plenty of work in Laos until the cease-fire there on

February 23. Shortly before the Laotian cease-fire, the repatriation of American prisoners began.

After the cease-fire in Laos, Cambodia suddenly became the only active battle ground in all of Southeast Asia. This had two results. First, communist forces began infiltrating Cambodia in greater numbers. The Khmer Rouge (Cambodian communists) had grown to become an effective force and enemy operations against the forces of the Khmer Republic increased significantly. Second, all air assets that had been used in Laos and Vietnam suddenly became available to the Rustics in Cambodia. Blue Chip was still running things from Seventh Air Force in Saigon, but was in the process of moving to Nakhon Phanom in Thailand. They were increasing the number of fighter and gunship sorties and taxing the ability of the Rustics to handle them.

The Rustic's parent unit, the Twenty-third TASS at Nakhon Phanom began rotating their Nail FACs to Ubon to help the Rustics. This created a minor problem as most of the Nails' work had been over the Ho Chi Minh trail in Laos. They had seldom worked directly with friendly ground commanders and troops-in-contact (TIC) situations. Also, the Nails were not familiar with the Cambodian geography or tactical situation and few of them spoke French. The Nails were outstanding FACs, though, and fast learners. They mastered their new mission quickly.

Because of the additional air assets, the Cambodian army was able to keep Route 4 open from Phnom Penh to Kompong Som, which improved Phnom Penh's supply situation and provided plenty of business for the Rustics and Nails.

March 1973 saw another improvement in Rustic operations. Lt. Col. Mark Berent, the air attaché at the American embassy in Phnom Penh, arranged for the Rustics to routinely land at Phnom Penh to refuel. There was no longer any secrecy about the air operation in Cambodia and no reason not to land at Phnom Penh. These were called "Phnom Penh Turns" and significantly increased the Rustics' on-station time. The flying time from Ubon to the Phnom Penh area was about an hour and fifteen minutes each way and refueling at Phnom Penh saved about two and a half hours of nonproductive travel. Sustained support of operations along Route 4 to Kompong Som would have been almost impossible without refueling at Phnom Penh.

The airport at Phnom Penh was something of a problem. It was poorly maintained and the runway was full of potholes and debris. The embassy laid down strict rules on how many U.S. personnel could be on the ground there at any one time and it was not uncommon for one Rustic to be orbiting the airport waiting for another Rustic to get airborne and make room for him.

At Phnom Penh, the Cambodian Air Force took care of refueling the OV-10 while the pilot found some shade and ate a Cambodian box lunch. The contents of the lunch box were never accurately determined. They were referred to as "monkey balls and rice" and eaten anyway.

In April 1973, the Rustics suffered a major loss when Rustic 07, 1st Lt. Joe Gambino was shot down near Kompong Thom. He was flying solo and working with the ground commander in that area, Brig. Gen. Teap Ben. According to witnesses, Joe's OV-10 was hit by automatic weapons, probably 12.7mm machine guns, and caught fire. He ejected at low altitude and his parachute opened, but he did not survive the landing. A Cambodian platoon recovered his body, which was draped in a Cambodian flag and returned to Ubon that same day. A service honoring Joe was held the next day at the Ubon chapel and his body was loaded onto a C-130 for the first leg of his trip home to New York City.

The Cambodians took the loss hard and their sorrow could be heard in the voices of their radio operators; particularly Sam's. Soon after Joe's death, Lt. Col. Bill Ernst, the Rustic commander, received a letter from Brig. Gen. Teap Ben.

> Monsieur the Lieutenant Colonel:
> On the occasion of the cruel loss of Lieutenant Joe Gambino, who died tragically the Seventh of April, 1973, on the field of honor of Kompong Thom: in the name of the officers, noncommissioned officers, soldiers, civil servants, civilian population, and in my own name, permit me to express to you as well as to the family of the regrettably lost, who has valiantly fought on our side for the cause of the Khmer Republic, my saddest condolences. The Khmer Republic, and in particular the Province of Kompong Thom, has lost in the person of Lieutenant Joe Gambino, a sincere friend and brave companion-in-arms. Be assured, Monsieur the Lieutenant Colonel, the assurances of my highest consideration. (Signed) Brigadier General Teap Ben.

During this time period, Lt. Col. Kohn Oum returned from the United States and became the commander of the Cambodian T-28 "Scorpions" and the Chief of Base Operations at Phnom Penh's Pochentong Airport.

In May, Lt. Col. Bill Powers replaced Bill Ernst as the Rustic Commander. Bill Powers left within a month and Maj. Si Dahle took his place. Major Dahle was the last Rustic Commander.

Ned Helm, Rustic 15, managed to make the news in early July 1973. He was working with a set of A-7s just east of Phnom Penh when the lead A-7 suddenly broke off the attack and started heading west, apparently NORDO (no radio) as he wasn't answering any of his wingman's calls. The A-7s had FM radios and Ned was able to contact him on the tactical FM frequency. He had lost all oil pressure and had decided to spend the night in Phnom Penh instead of under a tree with his parachute.

Ned called Pochentong tower and told them an A-7 was inbound for an immediate emergency landing. Ned also headed for Phnom Penh and told the A-7 wingman to terminate the attack and follow him. He then called Scorpion Ops to advise the air attaché (Mark Berent) that he was about to have a visitor. Mark was spending enough time at Pochentong Airport to deserve his own office.

The A-7 landed safely and taxied to a revetment. With everything under control, Ned and the A-7 wingman went back to work on the target.

When Ned was done with his first mission, he landed at Phnom Penh for fuel and lunch. After parking, he noted that the parked A-7 wasn't showing any obvious signs of an oil leak. The problem was probably failure of the oil pressure transmitter or the pressure gage itself. With a jet engine, though, total loss of oil was usually followed by severe engine failure within a minute or two. The pilots flying single engine jets tended to take the oil pressure indicator seriously.

Ned wandered into flight operations to pick up his lunch and talk to the Scorpion Ops Officer, Major Kahn, who told him to call Blue Chip in Saigon. Blue Chip canceled the second half of his double mission and told him to fly the A-7 pilot back to his base at Korat.

Eventually, Mark Berent and Mike Lang, the A-7 pilot, came in and Ned explained the change in plans. He and Mike went out to the OV-10 for the requisite lecture on the plane's ejection seat, canopy, radios, and so on. Ned hooked up Mike's harness for him and got the Koch fittings attached from the seat.[7] Mike was a very large person, and both were skeptical about whether he could safely eject or not. Ned also gave him specific instructions on closing the right canopy hatch and making sure it was locked. If not locked, it would come off in flight and scare everyone.

Ned fired up the engines and headed for the runway for takeoff. At about 600 feet above the ground, he heard a loud "bang" and the plane rolled viciously to the left. He pulled both throttles to idle and noted that the left engine had failed and the propeller auto-feathered. The right engine was not running well, but it was still putting out power. Ned turned left (which the plane wanted to do anyway), back to the airport, and punched the jettison button to get rid of the belly tank and rocket pods. Nothing happened. He pulled the manual jettison handle and that also did nothing. He was stuck with a plane that absolutely would not maintain altitude with an engine shut down and no way to get rid of all the weight and drag hanging beneath it. Ejection was beginning to look like a real possibility. He looked in his rearview mirror and he could see what had happened. Mike's right canopy hatch was gone and the left engine had probably eaten it.

Realizing that Mike might not survive an ejection, Ned told him to hang on and get a good grip on the seat handles. If things turned really hopeless, Ned could initiate the ejection for both of them from the front seat. About then the electrical system failed leaving them without radios.

They were on downwind leg to the runway, but still losing altitude. Ned bent the plane around in a tight left turn and landed right over the top of an AU-24, which had also just landed. The landing rollout was uneventful except for the heavy breathing from both seats. After parking, the Nail FAC commander, Howie Pierson, wandered up and commented that Ned really shouldn't demonstrate single-engine approaches in a combat zone with an unqualified passenger on board. He was kidding, of course, but his sense of humor broke

Sam (Sam Sok) and Rick Scaling at Pochentong Airport, Phnom Penh, 1973. Mark Berent collection.

the tension. Ned and Mike were both ferried home in other aircraft. Mike decided that he really didn't care much for the OV-10.

Because of the condition of the Pochentong runway, the pilots were leery of both takeoff and landing. One day, shortly after Ned Helm's emergency, Rick Scaling, Rustic 09, demonstrated why. He had finished his lunch and was back in his plane, fully fueled, and thundering down the runway on takeoff. Suddenly his left main tire hit something on the runway and blew out. Rick was not up to flying speed yet, and the plane was not going to accelerate with a blown tire. The OV-10 veered left off the runway into the grass and headed for a dirt berm along the airport access road. Rick used full brakes and full reverse on both engines, but the brakes weren't very effective on grass, particularly with one tire blown. Rick didn't think he could get the plane stopped and he was running out of options. Considering all the munitions and the 230 gallons of fuel in the belly tank beneath him, ejecting suddenly looked like a very good idea.

The marvelous LW-3B ejection seat and parachute worked perfectly and Rick landed unhurt. So did the OV-10. It rolled into a small rut in the ground

Results of Ned Helm's landing with nose gear failure and fire at Phnom Penh. Note failed nose landing gear in the foreground. Mark Berent collection.

and stopped a few feet from the berm with both engines still whining away in reverse. Rick walked over to it, reached in through the broken canopy, and shut off the engines. Mark Berent, the embassy air attaché, was at the airport and saw the whole thing. He went out and helped Rick gather up his parachute.

Rick spent the night in a Phnom Penh hotel and dined that evening with Sam (Hotel 21's radio operator). Sam happened to be visiting his family and heard about Rick's adventure. Four days later, the OV-10 was flying again with a new ejection seat, canopy and tire.

About then, early July, 1973, President Nixon announced the date for termination of all U.S. air activities in Southeast Asia: August 15, 1973. The days of the Rustics were numbered and the Phnom Penh Turns continued right up until the final day.

A few days after Rick Scaling's ejection at Phnom Penh, Ned Helm was again in the news. Phnom Penh was effectively under siege and the Khmer Rouge were making a strong effort to capture both the city and the airport. There was plenty of air support available, and Ned was at 10,000 feet over

Lt. Col. Mark Berent, Air Attaché, United States Embassy, Phnom Penh, and Cambodian (Khmer) friends. Mark Berent collection.

Phnom Penh acting as the "High FAC." The fighters would check in with him and he would brief them and park them in orbit until the "Low FAC" was ready for them. This system was a very efficient way to manage large numbers of fighters.

After about an hour and a half of this, his number one (left) engine failed and auto-feathered without warning. He was having his second single-engine landing experience within a week. He had plenty of altitude and flew a "textbook" engine-out pattern to the Pochentong runway. He landed on the main gear with no problem. When he lowered the nose wheel to the runway, it collapsed and all of a sudden he was skidding down the runway on the main landing gear and the belly tank. His escort (a Nail FAC in another OV-10) told him he was on fire. Ejection was not an option, as the ejection seat wouldn't go straight up because of the collapsed nose gear. Ned rode it out and dove out of the cockpit as soon as he could get untangled from all the straps holding him in. A Cambodian fire truck pulled up and extinguished the belly tank fuel fire. Ned managed to get away with only a sprained ankle, a sore back, and a new nickname—from then on he was known as "Crash" Helm.

One of the first on the scene was Mark Berent who had been beside the runway taking pictures of Ned's landing. That eliminated a lot of discussion about the quality of the landing. Investigation revealed a half-inch hole going in and out of the nose gear landing strut. Ned had been potted by a 12.7mm gun while on final approach with the landing gear down. Case closed.

The volume of Rustic and Nail operations at Pochentong airport remained high and the number of aircraft needing maintenance or repair was taxing the resources of the Twenty-third TASS at NKP and their Rustic Operating Location at Ubon. Because of the attacks on the airport by the Khmer Rouge, leaving an OV-10 parked there overnight merely provided "bait" for the attackers. Nevertheless, the Rustics kept up a full schedule and lost no planes to ground attacks at the airport.

12

The Final Rustic Missions

By the summer of 1973, it seemed to many that the fall of Phnom Penh and the rest of Cambodia was likely if not inevitable.[1] The Khmer Rouge were emerging as a potent force and American air support was not going to be available much longer. A cease-fire had been established in both Vietnam and Laos, but there was still intense fighting in Cambodia and the Rustics were as busy as ever. Congressional criticism was mounting, though, and President Nixon realized that if he didn't offer Congress a timetable for withdrawal from Cambodia, they were likely to require an immediate halt to all actions there. If he attempted to veto any such legislation, it would be overturned. In June, Nixon informed the Congress that he would not oppose legislation calling for a halt of the bombing in Cambodia in forty-five days, on the fifteenth of August. Congress accepted that and, on July 1, passed Public Law 93-52, which cut off all funds "to finance directly or indirectly combat activities by United States military forces in or over or from off the shores of South Vietnam, Laos or Cambodia." Nixon signed the bill that same day. Suddenly the Rustics knew exactly when it would all be over. It would officially end at noon, Cambodian time, on August 15, 1973. At that time, all American combat planes had to be out of Cambodia.

Although it had nothing to do with the Rustics, there was to be one more air disaster in Cambodia. Clandestine B-52 strikes had been used during 1969 and early 1970 inside the border of Cambodia to interdict the Ho Chi Minh trail. With the incursion into Cambodia in April 1970, those strikes were halted. As soon as Cambodia was accepted as an ally and air support procedures were established, the B-52s returned sporadically to Cambodia to strike enemy strongholds in areas where there were no friendly forces or population centers. The procedures were that the Cambodia military staff in Phnom Penh would select the targets and Seventh Air Force would approve them based on their knowledge of enemy activities. The Rustics were not involved, because there were no friendly forces involved. The Rustics seldom knew when or where the B-52s would strike.

After the cease fire in Vietnam and Laos, there were more B-52s available to strike Cambodian targets and the number of strikes increased significantly.

The B-52 radar bombing system required an identifiable aiming point that could be seen on their radar. If the target itself could be identified on radar, it could be bombed directly. If not, a nearby identifiable point could be used. This was called an offset aiming point (OAP) and the north-south and east-west distances from the OAP to the target would be set into the bombing computer. The radar bombing cross hairs would be placed on the OAP, but the bombs would actually be dropped on the target. This was very accurate providing the system was in "offset" mode. If the system was in "direct" mode, the bombs would be dropped where the crosshairs were placed.

In Cambodia, the targets themselves were seldom identifiable on radar. The common solution to this was to place a small battery-powered radar beacon at a known location so that the B-52s could use the beacon as the OAP. One such beacon was placed in the town of Neak Luong, which was a ferry crossing southeast of Phnom Penh.[2] The actual target was several miles away.

On August 6, 1973, a B-52 dropped 20 tons of bombs on the radar beacon and Neak Luong because the bomber's system was in "direct" mode instead of "offset" mode. There were four hundred casualties, both killed and wounded. It was a bomb delivery error and there was nothing anyone outside of the B-52 could have done to prevent it.

Nevertheless, one result of this was that Colonel Oum (who had returned from Taiwan) got involved in the development of a Direct Air Support Center (DASC) at the Cambodian Air Force (KAF) headquarters in Phnom Penh. This was primarily because no one else had his knowledge of needed communications equipment. While involved in that, Colonel Oum met USAF Lt. Col. Dave Sands, who had been sent from Seventh Air Force to help set up the DASC. Dave would later sponsor Colonel Oum and his family for residence in the United States.

The Cambodian chief of staff wanted Oum to run the Direct Air Support Center, but he declined. He knew that whoever ran it had to be from the Air

Force and have some knowledge of aviation. Although Oum started his career as an Air Force communications officer, most of his current training was from the Army General Staff College in Cambodia. His expertise was in ground warfare. Oum had one other problem with being in charge of a major operation: Corruption in Phnom Penh was rampant and getting worse.

"They cannot keep me there for I was very straight. I am not a crook, so if I see something wrong, I have to say something. So they say, 'OK, we send you to Bangkok (Thailand) to be Defense Attaché.' I say, 'OK, that's nice.' "

Meanwhile, the final date of August 15 moved inexorably closer. The Rustics were determined to finish strong and have planes in the air over Cambodia right up until the last minute. On August 14, the day before the cessation of all air activities, the Rustics flew the final "Phnom Penh Turn." Randy Hetherington (Rustic 18) and Jon Wroblewski (Nail 58) launched from Ubon with Randy in the front seat. They flew a support mission for the ground commander at Kompong Cham and recovered at Phnom Penh for fuel and lunch.

The final combat flight of the Rustics and the Nails, August 15, 1973. The pilots were (Lead) Howie Pierson and Bob Negley, (Two) Charlie Yates and Woody Baker, (Three) Bill Powers and Wayne Wroten, and (Four) Darrell Whitcomb and Bob Haley. Si Dahle collection.

While there, we visited with the local commander who was anxious about tomorrow being the last day of American air support. We assured him that the Cambodian Air Force could handle the air support and that if things got really bad, we would come back. That speech got me a hug, a handshake, and a temple-rubbing from Angkor Wat as a gift. When we got back to the plane, Jon took the front seat and we took off for our next mission. Since I was in the backseat, I can say that the last American FAC out of Phnom Penh was a Rustic.

The next day, the combined Rustic/Nail operation flew thirty-one sorties before the noon deadline. A Nail FAC was the last U.S. Forward Air controller to expend ordnance in Cambodia. The U.S. Air Force officially credited an A-7 fighter pilot based in Thailand with dropping the last bomb, marking an end to the nation's longest war. Perhaps so, but he did it under the supervision of a FAC.

The last four Rustic/Nail OV-10s joined in formation and crossed the Cambodian border outbound at exactly noon. At Ubon, they flew a "missing man" formation down the runway before peeling off and landing. There was a celebration, but not a very big one. They knew they were abandoning friends who needed their help and were not likely to survive without it.

On September 10, 1973, Capt. Tom Yarborough (Rustic 21) led the last three Rustic OV-10s from Ubon to Nakhon Phanom, where they were deactivated.

That was the last time the Rustic call sign was used.

It was over.

Epilogue

That was the end of the Rustic operation, but not quite the end of American involvement in Cambodia.

With the withdrawal of American air support, the ability of the Khmer Republic to survive was considered doubtful. The NVA was beginning to pull out of Cambodia in order to help with the final push to take total control of South Vietnam. The Khmer Rouge was continuing to grow stronger. Their leader, Saloth Sar, emerged under the name of Pol Pot[1] and conducted regular artillery and rocket attacks on Phnom Penh. In reality, Lon Nol's Khmer Republic controlled very little territory outside of Phnom Penh.

In November 1973, a plan called Tactical Air Improvement Plan, Cambodia, was developed and USAF Brig. Gen. Harry C. (Heinie) Aderholt was put in charge of it. He operated from Bangkok, Thailand, and among his first acts was suppling the Cambodians with more aircraft, primarily T-28s and helicopters, and bringing the aircraft they had to Thailand for much-needed maintenance. He also set up a training program in Thailand for Cambodian pilots.

Heinie Aderholt also took on the problem of moving supplies to Cambodia. River convoys were out. There was no air cover and the U.S. Navy was no longer available to organize them in South Vietnam. USAF C-130s were still flying airdrop missions to Cambodia from U Tapao, Thailand, but the total cargo moved was small compared to the needs. Because of the political ramifications of loss of a C-130 over Cambodia, General Aderholt recommended that a civilian contractor take over the supply mission using unmarked USAF

C-130 aircraft. Birdair, a division of Bird & Sons, was a contractor that had been operating for years in that part of the world and was acceptable to both the U.S. Air Force and the Thai government. By the time of its termination in 1975, the supply airlift had grown to be the largest since the Berlin airlift in 1948–1949. The story of that support is well told in Gen. Heinie Aderholt's biography.[2]

The Lon Nol regime held out until 1975 and made a series of offers to negotiate with the Khmer Rouge. None of them were accepted.[3] In April, the government of the Khmer Republic collapsed and Lon Nol and his family left Cambodia. By April 10, most Americans and the embassy staff had been evacuated to Thailand. The American Embassy closed on April 12.[4]

Although everyone was expecting a massive attack on Phnom Penh by the Khmer Rouge, it didn't happen. On April 17, two weeks before the fall of Saigon, the Khmer Rouge just marched into the city and took over the government buildings. They established Democratic Kampuchea under the leadership of Pol Pot and ordered the immediate evacuation of everyone from Phnom Penh. This was the beginning of the genocide action in which, by some estimates, more than a million Cambodians were slaughtered.

In May 1975, Khmer Rouge naval forces boarded and captured an American cargo ship, the *Mayaguez*, in international waters in the Gulf of Thailand. Since there were no lines of communication between the United States and the Khmer Rouge, President Ford approved a naval bombardment of Kompong Som and an armed assault against the island where the *Mayaguez* was being held. In actuality, the *Mayaguez* crew had already been released before the assault began. The assault cost the American navy and marines over eighty casualties, both killed and wounded, and the loss of four helicopters.[5] Some OV-10s from Nakhon Phanom flew missions in support of that action, but they were not Rustics.

Some other loose ends need tying off.

Col. Lieou Phin Oum and his family were already in Thailand and entered the American refugee program. With the help and sponsorship of Lt. Col. Dave Sands and some of the Rustics, including Col. Ray Stratton, Colonel Oum and his entire family were evacuated to the United States and settled in Austin, Texas. Dave was the commander of an O-2 squadron at nearby Bergstrom AFB and affiliated with a church group who could officially act as sponsor. Dave and his church group provided Oum and his family with a fully furnished home, clothes, food, and entry into the community. Oum used his skills in communications to earn a living, and all of his children entered school and earned college degrees, most of them in technical fields.

Capt. San Sok (Sam) disappeared and managed to make his own way to the United States as a refugee. He located Mark Berent, who was able to help him. He worked at various jobs in the United States but eventually returned to Cambodia, where he now lives a few kilometers from Kompong Thom.

Lt. Col. Kohn Om, after the Rustics left, was sent to Battambang as commandant of the Air Force Academy. By mid-1974, he was back in Phnom Penh as the deputy chief of Air Force Intelligence. He continued to fly as a pilot and had every opportunity to escape in 1975. He might even have crammed his family into a T-28 and brought them with him—many Cambodian pilots did that. As he put it, "I couldn't throw away my country just to save my life." In a story that deserves to be a book itself, he and his family walked to the Vietnamese border and settled in a small Vietnamese community as farmers. Since exit visas were nearly impossible to obtain, he decided to go back across Cambodia to Thailand and attempt to enter the United States as a refugee. During that trip, he was captured by the Khmer Rouge. He managed to escape and made his way to a refugee camp across the border in Thailand. In Bangkok, he met Mark Berent,[6] who he had known as the air attaché at the U.S. Embassy in Phnom Penh. Mark vouched for him and met him when he finally arrived at Dulles Airport in Washington, D.C. With some help from the American Ambassador to the United Nations, Jean Kirkpatrick, and the former Secretary of Defense, Melvin Laird, travel from Vietnam was arranged for his family. In 1986, eleven years after escaping from Cambodia, his family finally arrived in the United States. Kohn Om and his family are now American citizens and live in Virginia.

Dung Ngoc Le ("June," the Night Rustic maid at Bien Hoa) made it to the United States as a refugee and now lives with her husband and children in Virginia.

Missue, the Rustic mascot, was brought (some might say smuggled) to the United States by one of the Rustic backseaters and lived in luxury to a ripe old age.

Mark Berent retired from the Air Force and became a successful author in his own right. He lives in Arizona.

The Rustics scattered to the four corners of the country and beyond. Some stayed in the Air Force until retirement. Many stayed in the aviation field and several became airline pilots. In 1995, the Rustics began rediscovering each other and formed the Rustic FAC Association. They learned that there was no official history of the Rustic operation, so they began collecting information on it. This book is one of the products of that process.

Today, Cambodia has enjoyed a few years of stability in its government and its economy is slowly beginning to recover from the ravages of Pol Pot, the Khmer Rouge, and the North Vietnamese. There are efforts to attract investment and tourists are gradually returning. In November 2000, some of the Rustics went back to Cambodia to visit places they knew very well from the air and meet people they knew only as voices on the radio. One of the objectives of the Rustic FAC Association is to aid Cambodian relief and assist that country in its efforts to restore its civilization. For those wishing more information, the Rustic website is www.rustic.org.

If nothing else, the war in Cambodia showed that massive airpower cannot compensate for a basically weak ground force. The Cambodians were overmatched and the United States could not put troops on the ground to help them.

It is hard to think of anything good to say about the war in Southeast Asia, but the friendships the Rustics established in Cambodia and their efforts in behalf of that country were a small entry on the plus side of the ledger. For almost all of us, that was the most memorable and satisfying period of our military careers.

Jim Reese (Rustic 57) describes the feeling many of us carry:

> I was still a second lieutenant, fresh out of flying school. There I was, going through FAC training with orders to Vietnam in my hand. One night we had a party and one of our flight instructors, a combat veteran, had a couple of drinks and began to get a little melancholy.
>
> "I really envy you young pilots. You're about to begin your combat flying assignment in Vietnam. Enjoy it, because it's the best assignment you'll have in your entire Air Force career."
>
> I did not want to hear that! I hadn't even begun my Air Force career. Did he mean that after this it was all downhill? That the rest of my Air Force career would be boring and purposeless by comparison? That couldn't possibly be true.
>
> But, of course, it was true.

Appendix
The Rustics

Name	Position	Aircraft	Call Sign	Rustic Tour Dates
Adams, Thomas B. (Tom)	pilot	O-2/OV-10	01	Jan. 71–Aug. 71
Aitken, Douglas B. (Doug)	pilot	OV-10	16	May 71–May 72
Andrews, Robert P. (Bob)	pilot	OV-10	07	Sep. 71–Sep. 72
Arellano, Walter J.	pilot	O-2	01	Jul. 71–Oct. 71
Atkins, Benny J. (Ben)	pilot	OV-10	02	Dec. 71–Jul. 72
Atwater, Robert S. (Bob)	pilot	O-2		Nov. 70–May 71
Auth, Jerry	pilot	O-2		Jun. 70–Nov. 70
Babin, Gabriel	interpreter	OV-10		
Bahr, Chip	maintenance			
Baker, Joseph W.	pilot	OV-10	12	Nov. 72–Aug. 73
Baker, Noel W. (Wayne)	pilot	O-2	22	Jun. 70–Jun. 71
Ball, Gary A.	pilot	OV-10	13	Mar. 73-Aug. 73
Ballard, Michael W. (Mike)	pilot	OV-10	16	Aug. 72–Jul. 73
Barazzotto, Richard A. (Zot)	pilot	OV-10	55	Dec. 70–Jan. 71
Bell, Glen L., Jr.	pilot	O-2	28	Aug. 70–Mar. 71
Bellefueille, Gil B.	interpreter	O-2/OV-10	Tango	Aug. 70–Nov. 71
Bennett, Bill	maintenance	OV-10		Oct. 72–Aug. 73
Bergeron, Joseph L. (Lee)	pilot	OV-10		Jan. 71–Jan. 72
Blais, Roger D.	interpreter	OV-10		
Boggess, Edward M. (Ed)	radio operator			Oct. 71–Feb. 72
Borah, Steve B.	pilot	O-2		Oct. 70–Oct. 71
Boston, Jeffrey A. (Jeff)	pilot	O-2	51	Dec. 70–May 71
Bowen, Jack E.	pilot	O-2	32	Apr. 71–Jul. 71
Boyle, Joseph E. (Jay)	pilot	OV-10		Jul. 72–Jul. 73
Brooks, Don L.	pilot	OV-10	02	Jul. 70–Dec. 70
Brower, George	pilot	OV-10	02 /12	Aug. 70–Jan. 71

Continued on next page

Name	Position	Aircraft	Call Sign	Rustic Tour Dates
Brown, Howard D. (Rocky)	maintenance	OV-10		Jul. 71–Jul. 72
Brunelle, Emil H.	interpreter	OV-10	Foxtrot	Dec. 70–Sep. 71
Burgoyne, Robert C. (Bob)	interpreter	OV-10	Zulu	Jun. 70–Mar. 71
Calvanelli, Thomas J. (Tom)	pilot	OV-10	11/61	Mar. 71–Jul. 71
Canter, Thomas H. (Tom)	pilot	O-2	31	Nov. 70–Sep. 71
Capps, Thomas E. (Tom)	pilot	OV-10	12	May 71–Dec. 71
Carruthers, William (Bill), Jr.	pilot	O-2	34	Sep. 70–Aug. 71
Cary, John F.	pilot	OV-10	01	Nov. 71–Dec. 71
Case, Thomas R. (Tom)	pilot	O-2	30	Jun. 71–Jun. 72
Casey, Charles W. (Chuck)	pilot	O-2	35	Apr. 71–Sep. 71
Caywood, Douglas E. (Doug)	pilot	OV-10	17	Jul. 72–Jul. 73
Centilla, Robert	pilot	OV-10		
Chang, Standley	interpreter			
Charlton, John T.	pilot	OV-10	23	Sep. 71–Sep. 72
Cimon, Norman J.	interpreter	OV-10		
Clifford, Robert R. (Bob)	pilot	OV-10	03	Nov. 70–Nov. 71
Clinch, Thomas P. (Tom)	pilot	OV-10	18	May 71–Jun. 72
Cooper, Harry	intelligence			
Cross, Stephen D. (Steve)	pilot	O-2	28	Jun. 71–Sep. 71
Crumpler, Swanson R. (Rae)	maintenance	OV-10		71–72
Currier, Louis F. (Lou)	pilot	OV-10	09	Jun. 70–Nov. 70
Czarnecki, Damien	pilot	O-2	47	Aug. 71
Dahle, Simend E. (Si)	pilot	OV-10	11	Sep. 72–Aug. 73
Dandeneau, Ronald J. (Ron)	interpreter	OV-10	Foxtrot	Jun. 70–Dec. 70
Davenport, Michael R. (Mike)	pilot	O-2	17	Jun. 70–Mar. 71
Decabooter, William R. (Bill)	pilot	OV-10	05	Aug. 72–Mar. 73
Dekoker, David J. (Zeke)	pilot	O-2	32	Jul. 70–May 71
Deshaise, Roland L. (Deke)	interpreter	OV-10	Yankee	
Dimmick, Paul H., Jr.	pilot	O-2	39	Jul. 70–Jun. 71
Dodd, Roger H.	pilot	OV-10	07	Jun. 70–Dec. 70
Dodd, Walter O. (Waldo)	pilot	OV-10	19	Jun. 71–Dec. 71
Dorr, Donald S. (Don)	intelligence		Delta	Aug. 70–Jul. 71
Dow, Ralph E.	interpreter	OV-10	Delta	Aug. 71–Aug. 72
Doyon, Jean Paul	interpreter	OV-10	Oscar	
Driskill, Larry W.	pilot	O-2	35	Jun. 70–May 71
Drury, Johnny B.	pilot	OV-10	04	Jan. 71–Dec. 71
Dufresne, Joseph R. G. (Jerry)	interpreter	O-2/OV-10	India	Jun. 70–Feb. 71
Early, Timothy E.	interpreter	OV-10		
Eby, Tim	pilot	OV-10	40	Aug. 70
Echelberger, Arthur D. (Don)	pilot	OV-10	10	Jun. 72–Jun. 73
Eddy, Garrett E.*	pilot	O-2	23	Jun. 70–Oct. 70
Edmonson, William Larry	pilot	OV-10	05	Jul. 71–Jan. 72
Edwards, Lendy C.	pilot	OV-10	20	Apr. 72–Oct. 72
Eklund, Roy E.	interpreter	O-2/OV-10	Oscar	Feb. 71–Oct. 71
Ellis, Donald L. (Don)	pilot	OV-10	17	Nov. 70–Jun. 71

Name	Position	Aircraft	Call Sign	Rustic Tour Dates
Ernst, William L. (Bill)	pilot	OV-10	04	May 72–May 73
Engleman, John (Johnny)	pilot	OV-10	03	Jul. 70–Nov. 70
Evans, King Charles (KC)		O-2		Jul. 70–Jan. 71
Falcon, Normand	interpreter	OV-10	Quebec	Jun. 70–May 71
Fink, Carl		O-2		Jul. 70–Nov. 70
Franklin, Arnold L. (Arnie), Jr.	pilot	OV-10	22	Oct. 71
Freix, Greg D.	pilot	OV-10	18	Aug. 70–Jun. 71
Frey, Hans G.	interpreter	OV-10	Foxtrot	Jan. 72–Dec. 72
Friedhofen, Walter, L. (Walt)	interpreter	OV-10	Romeo	Aug. 70–Nov. 71
Frischmuth, Phillip A. (Phil)	pilot	OV-10	55	Jan. 71–Dec. 71
Gabel, James A. (Jim)	intelligence		Bravo	Jun. 70–Jun. 71
Gagne, Michael J. (Mike)	interpreter	OV-10	Kilo	Jul. 70–Dec. 70
Gaida, Jerry A.	munitions	OV-10		Jul. 70–Sep. 70
Galland, Joseph A.	interpreter			
Gamache, Ronald G. (Ron)	interpreter	O-2/OV-10	Victor	Aug. 70–May 71
Gambino, Joseph, Jr.*	pilot	OV-10	07	Apr. 73
Garand, Joseph A. E. (Joe)	interpreter	OV-10	Echo	Aug. 71–Jun. 72
Gaskill, Simond P. (Si)	pilot	OV-10	09	Sep. 70–Mar. 71
Gestas, Jean Claude	interpreter	OV-10	X-ray	Oct. 71–Jul. 72
Gibbar, James M. (Mick)	pilot	O-2	25	Oct. 70–Sep. 71
Gibson, Lester (Les)	pilot	OV-10	01	Jul. 71–Jul. 72
Gilchrist, Michael H. (Mike)	pilot	O-2		Jun. 70–Jan. 71
Gill, Larry (Blackmax)	interpreter	O-2/OV-10	Yankee	Dec. 70–Nov. 71
Goddard, Richard H. (Dick)	pilot	OV-10	20	Feb. 73-Aug. 73
Gonzales, H. R. Damon	pilot	O-2	46	Jun. 71–Jun. 72
Grattopp, Ronald A. (Ron)	pilot	O-2	44	May 71–Sep. 71
Green, Richard C. (Dick)	pilot	OV-10	23	Feb. 71–Jul. 71
Greene, Charles D. (Goose)	pilot	O-2	21	Nov. 70–Sep. 71
Gregg, Scott	pilot	O-2		Dec. 70
Haas, William	pilot	O-2		Jun. 70–Sep. 70
Hagle, Donald H. (Don)	pilot	O-2	40	Jun. 70–Jun. 71
Haller, Donald S. (Don)	pilot	OV-10	18	Apr. 71–Jun. 71
Hamann, Roger J.	interpreter	OV-10	Yankee	Oct. 71–Aug. 72
Harris, Robert, N. (Bob)	pilot	O-2	33	Dec. 70–Sep. 71
Harshaw, Robert G. (Bob)	pilot	OV-10	15	Jun. 72–Apr. 73
Hawker, Curtis O. (Curt)	pilot	OV-10	06	Sep. 72–Aug. 73
Hawley, Jon A.	pilot	OV-10	13	Apr. 72–Feb. 73
Healey, William P. (Bill)	pilot	O-2		
Hein, David	pilot	OV-10		
Hellwig, Douglas E.	pilot	OV-10	14	Jul. 70–Mar. 71
Helm, Henry E. (Ned)	pilot	OV-10	15	Apr. 73-Aug. 73
Hetherington, James R. (Jim)	pilot	O-2/OV-10	02	Jun. 70–Feb. 71
Hetherington, Randy W.	pilot	OV-10	18	Feb. 73-Aug. 73
Hopkins, Steven V. (Steve)	pilot	O-2	45	Nov. 70–Sep. 71

Continued on next page

Name	Position	Aircraft	Call Sign	Rustic Tour Dates
Hughes, W. Larry (Chance)	munitions	O-2/OV-10		Jun. 70–Jul. 71
Hull, David D. (Dave)	pilot	O-2	29	Jun. 70–Feb. 71
Inman, Brownie N.	pilot	OV-10		Jan. 72–Dec. 72
Jamrosy, Tom	pilot	O-2	30	Mar. 71–Jun. 71
Jessup, Robert H. (Jess)	pilot	OV-10	13	Jan. 71–Dec. 71
Johnson, Michael	pilot	OV-10		
Jones, Thomas M. (Tom)	pilot	O-2	54	Nov. 70–Sep. 71
Joy, Steve	pilot	O-2		Jul. 70–Jun. 71
Keese, Henry B. (Hank)	pilot	OV-10	16	Sep. 70–Apr. 71
Kimbell, Earl S. (Shad), Jr.	pilot	OV-10	10	Jun. 71–Jun. 72
Kiraly, Emery M. (Mike)	pilot	OV-10	22	Apr. 73-Aug. 73
Kline, Tim	pilot	O-2		
Knox, Larry	pilot	O-2	28	Apr. 71
Koeppel, Ronald W. (Ron)	pilot	OV-10	09	Sep. 71–Sep. 72
Koppin, John A. (Jack)	pilot	O-2	02	Jan. 71–Aug. 71
Krueger, Walther A. (Walt), Jr.	pilot	O-2	13	Jun. 70–Jul. 70
Krupinski, Mark	pilot	OV-10		
Lancaster, Blake	pilot	O-2	38	Jun. 71–Sep. 71
Landtroop, Larry L.	pilot	O-2	43	Aug. 70–Feb. 71
Lanoue, Roger	interpreter	OV-10		Jul. 71–Jun. 72
Larson, George E. (Lunchbox)	interpreter	O-2/OV-10	Uniform	Aug. 70–Jul. 71
Lemke, William A. (Bill), Jr.	pilot	O-2	27	Sep. 70–Sep. 71
Lester, James W. (Jim)	pilot	OV-10	01	Jun. 70–Jan. 71
Lewis, Nicholas, L. (Nick)	interpreter	OV-10	Bravo	Sep. 71–Sep. 72
Leydorf, Bill	pilot	OV-10	10	Jun. 70–May 71
Life, Malcom L.	pilot	O-2		Jun. 70–Aug. 70
Ligondè, Pierre M.	interpreter	O-2/OV-10	Juliett	Aug. 70–Jul. 71
Lillis, Thomas M. (Tom)	pilot	O-2		Jun. 70–Dec. 70
Litton, John C.	pilot	O-2	42	Aug. 70–Dec. 70
Manuel, Charles R.	interpreter	OV-10		
Martin, Wilbur V. (Bill)		O-2		Jun. 70–Apr. 71
McAdams, William (Bill)	pilot	OV-10	21	Sep. 71–Sep. 72
McClellan, Jerry L.	pilot	OV-10	14	Sep. 71–Sep. 72
Mercer, Harold G. (Don)	pilot	O-2	41	Oct. 70–Sep. 71
Mesa, William C.	radio operator			
Messer, Robert D. (Bob)	pilot	O-2	24	Jun. 70–Jun. 71
Metcalf, Allen	pilot	OV-10		Aug. 70–Jun. 71
Mitchell, Douglas, J. (Doug)	pilot	OV-10	30	May 71–Apr. 72
Mittendorf, Ehrhard, III	pilot	O-2	49	Dec. 70–Feb. 71
Montmarquet, Robert M. (Bob)	interpreter	O-2/OV-10	Golf	Sep. 70–Oct. 71
Morneau, Marcel J.	interpreter	OV-10	Victor	Jul. 71–Jul. 72
Morneault, Phillip	interpreter	OV-10	Bravo	Jul. 71–Feb. 72
Morrison, Dave	pilot	O-2		Jan. 71–Mar. 71
Morton, William G. (Bill)	pilot	OV-10	10	Aug. 70–Dec. 70
Murphy, Clint J. A.	interpreter	O-2/OV-10	Charlie	Sep. 70–Sep. 71

Name	Position	Aircraft	Call Sign	Rustic Tour Dates
Newland, Claude G.	pilot	OV-10	19	Aug. 70–May 71
Norman, Carl D. (Doug)	interpreter	OV-10	Mike	May 71–May 72
Nuber, James (Nubes)	pilot	OV-10	05	Sep. 70–May 71
Om, Kohn	Cambodian pilot	T-28	Scorpion	
Osborn, Don				
Oum, Lieou Phin	Cambodian commander		Hotel 303	
Paquin, Joseph D. (Joe)	interpreter	O-2/OV-10	Sierra	Mar. 71–Sep. 71
Paradis, Arthur X. (Bob)	interpreter	OV-10	X-ray	Aug. 70–Jul. 71
Parsons, David S. (Dave)	pilot	OV-10	08	Jun. 70–Nov. 70
Peacock, Jeff	pilot	O-2		Mar. 71
Pells, G. Wendell	pilot	O-2	50	Aug. 70–Jul. 71
Perkins, Ben R.	pilot	O-2	31	Jul. 70–Nov. 70
Perry, Glen M., II	pilot	O-2	26	Nov. 70–Jul. 71
Polk, Chris	pilot	OV-10	56	Dec. 70–Aug. 71
Powers, William (Bill)	pilot	OV-10	01	May 73-Aug. 73
Ramielien, Oscar	interpreter	OV-10		
Ratledge, Dan	pilot	OV-10	64	Jan. 71–Dec. 71
Reese, James W. (Jim)	pilot	OV-10	57	Nov. 70–Apr. 71
Rember, Bill	intelligence			
Rheinhart, Richard (Dick)	pilot	OV-10	02	Jun. 70
Richards, Albert P. (Putt)	pilot	OV-10	14	Jan. 71–Oct. 71
Riehl, Paul A.	pilot	OV-10	06	Jun. 70–Dec. 70
Roberds, Richard M. (Dick)	pilot	O-2	21	Nov. 70–Sep. 71
Robertson, Douglas A.	radio operator			Aug. 71–Jul. 72
Ross, Milton C. (Milt)	pilot	O-2	42	Aug. 70–Feb. 71
Ryals, Robert (Bob)	pilot	OV-10	08	Dec. 72–Aug. 73
Safley, Jon G.	pilot	OV-10	19	Mar. 72–Dec. 72
San, Sok (Sam)	Cambodian radio operator		Hotel 21	
Scaling, Joseph R. (Rick)	pilot	OV-10	09	Sep. 72–Aug. 73
Schaum, Craig O.	pilot	OV-10	03	Jan. 71–Dec. 71
Schultz, Charles J.	interpreter	OV-10		
Schwein, Robert G. (Bob)	pilot	OV-10	20	Jun. 71–Dec. 71
Seibold, James C. (Jim)	pilot	OV-10	13	Aug. 70–Mar. 71
Shields, Merle R.	pilot	O-2	37	Nov. 70–Jul. 71
Shinafelt, Donald J. (Don)	pilot	OV-10	15	Jul. 70–Aug. 70
Sims, Arnold G	pilot	OV-10		Oct. 70–Jun. 71
Sleigh, William F. (Bill)	pilot	OV-10	12	Mar. 71–May 71
Smith, Charles, P.	interpreter	OV-10		
Smith, Walter L.	radio operator			
Sovich, Frank E.	pilot	O-2	36	Jun. 70–Apr. 71

Continued on next page

Name	Position	Aircraft	Call Sign	Rustic Tour Dates
Spencer, Joe P.	pilot	OV-10	06	Nov. 70–Sep. 71
St. John, Wayne	pilot	OV-10	08	Dec. 70–Aug. 71
Stearns, Michael L. (Mike)	pilot	OV-10		Feb. 72–Oct. 72
Stevenson, John R.	pilot	O-2		Jul. 70–Jun. 71
Stone, Donn E.	pilot	O-2	39	Jun. 70–Dec. 70
Storer, Harold S. (Shell), Jr.	pilot	OV-10	14	Dec. 72–Aug. 73
Stratton, Raymond E. (Ray)	pilot	OV-10	03	Jan. 72–Nov. 72
Strickland, Jack L.	pilot	O-2	38	Nov. 70– Feb. 71
Thomas, Robert F. (Doc)	doctor		X-ray 01	Dec. 70–Oct. 71
Thompson, John W. (Jack)	pilot	OV-10	11	Sep. 71–Sep. 72
Thrower, Michael B. (Mike)	pilot	O-2	34	Nov. 70–Mar. 71
Tisdale, Dave	intelligence			Dec. 70–Oct. 71
Trapp, Lansford E. (Lanny), Jr.	pilot	OV-10	07	Jan. 71–Nov. 71
Twaddell, James W. (Jim), III	pilot	OV-10	24	Feb. 72–Feb. 73
Underwood, Larry D. (Doc)	doctor		Doc	Oct. 71–Oct. 72
Vaillancourt, Joseph R. (Joe)	interpreter	OV-10	Hotel	Jun. 70–Feb. 71
Van Dyke, David C. (Dave)	pilot	OV-10	04	Jun. 70–Nov. 70
Van Kirk, Rodney W. (Ron)	pilot	OV-10	08	Jul. 71–Jun. 72
Vick, Terry T.	intelligence			Sep. 70–Sep. 71
Virnig, Thomas H.	intelligence			Dec. 70–Oct. 71
Virtue, Robert B. (Bob)	pilot	O-2	30	Jun. 70–Feb. 71
Voss, William E. (Bill)	intelligence			Jan. 71–Dec. 71
Vrablick, Michael S. (Mike)*	pilot	O-2		Aug. 70–Oct. 70
Wagner, Paul	pilot	OV-10		
Walinski, Carl O. (Otto)	pilot	V-10	15	Dec. 70–Dec. 71
Wenck, Ralph E.	intelligence			Jul. 70–Dec. 70
Williams, Gilbert L. (Gil)	pilot	OV-10	05	Feb. 71–Dec. 71
Wilson, William M. (Mike)	pilot	OV-10	08	Aug. 70–Mar. 71
Wilson, Paul P.	pilot	OV-10	17	
Winkler, George A. (Tony)		O-2		Aug. 71–Oct. 71
Wood, Richard H. (Dick)	pilot	OV-10	11	Jun. 70–Mar. 71
Wood, Wayne L.	pilot	OV-10	06	Sep. 71–Sep. 72
Wright, Randy	pilot	O-2		Dec. 70–Mar. 71
Yarborough, Thomas, R. (Tom)	pilot	OV-10	21	Nov. 72–Aug. 73

Note: All call signs are Rustic except for Cambodian call signs. This table was compiled by the Rustic FAC Association based on information submitted by their members.

* Killed in action

Notes

Prologue

1. During the German occupation of France in World War II, the Germans created a French government composed of German sympathizers, the Vichy French. The name came from the town the Germans selected as the seat of the French government.
2. Chandler, David P. *The Tragedy of Cambodian History: Politics, War, and Revolution since 1945* (New Haven: Yale University Press, 1991), 71, and William Shawcross, *Sideshow: Kissinger, Nixon and the Destruction of Cambodia* (New York: Simon and Schuster, 1981), 45–48.
3. Chandler, *The Tragedy of Cambodia*, 139–46; Shawcross, *Sideshow*, 61–67; Wilford P. Deac, *Road to the Killing Fields: The Cambodian War of 1970–1975* (College Station: Texas A&M University Press, 1997), 44; Craig Etcheson, *The Rise and Demise of Democratic Kampuchea* (Boulder, Colo.: Westview Press, 1984), 64. This explains why American bombing of the Ho Chi Minh trail in Laos seemed to have little effect on the supplies and munitions coming into South Vietnam.
4. Russell K. Ross, *Cambodia: A Country Study* (Washington, D.C.: U.S. Government Printing Office, 1990), *The Tragedy of Cambodia*, 113.
5. Chandler, *The Tragedy of Cambodia*, 168–71.
6. Ibid., 187. Instead of returning to Cambodia, Sihanouk had flown to Moscow to seek Russian help against the North Vietnamese and Viet Cong. Failing, he was on his way to the airport to depart for Beijing when he learned that Lon Nol had deposed him and had established the Khmer Republic.
7. Ibid.
8. Elizabeth Becker, *When the War Was Over: Cambodia and the Khmer Rouge Revolution* (New York: Public Affairs, Perseus Books Group, 1986; rev. 1998), 123.
9. Ibid., 14. Historian Becker argues that this was done without Lon Nol's knowledge. That's possible, but it seems unlikely. Within days of the "invasion" Cambodian Army and Air Force Officers were visiting Bien Hoa and Tan Son Nhut to learn American

tactics and coordinate operations. Cambodia's entire fleet of Russian MiG aircraft (six each, MiG 15s and MiG 17s) landed at Bien Hoa to be modified to carry American munitions.

1. The Birth of the Rustics

1. In Malaysian, "Kompong" translates as "village of" but in Cambodian it translates as "port of." It prefaces many Cambodian place names that are located on lakes, rivers, large streams, and the seacoast. Americans tended to drop the "Kompong," while Cambodians seldom dropped it. For consistency, it is used throughout the book whenever it is part of the place name.
2. Common aircraft radios are HF (High Frequency), VHF (Very High Frequency), and UHF (Ultra High Frequency.) VHF and UHF are "line of sight" radios, which means that the transmitter and the receiver must be able to "see" each other. HF radios bounce their transmissions off the ionosphere and are long-range radios. FAC aircraft also carried FM (frequency modulation) radios, which were short-range field radios used by army units on the ground.

2. The Backseaters

1. "G" refers to the force of gravity. In our normal lives, we are exposed to a force of 1 G. If we ride on a roller coaster at the amusement park, that force can be increased or decreased depending on whether we are at the bottom and starting back up or at the top and starting down. The G loads in aircraft can be quite high and pilots constantly exposed to them usually wear anti-G suits that inflate to keep blood from leaving the chest region and pooling in the legs. The OV-10 was capable of 8 positive and 3 negative G's, which is a lot more than roller coasters can deliver. OV-10 pilots normally fired marking rockets from about a 60-degree dive. After firing, the pilot would immediately pull back on the control stick and load the plane to about 6 positive G's. This put him in a 60-degree climb and, if he did it correctly, he could look back over his shoulder and see his smoke rocket hit. Although the plane was equipped for an anti-G suit, pilots seldom wore them. It was too hot and 6 G's for a few seconds was tolerable.
2. While pilots were assigned numbers for call signs, the backseaters were assigned letters. To pronounce the letter, they used the phonetic alphabet equivalent for that letter. The letter "C" was Charlie, "I" was India, "F" was Foxtrot and so on.
3. Tan Son Nhut had barracks, but living quarters anywhere else in Vietnam were called hooches.
4. A wafer switch is a rotary switch with several positions. It is somewhat analogous to the fan switch on many automobile heating systems. It was located on the left console of the OV-10 just behind the individual buttons that allowed selection and volume control of each radio and interphone. The backseater had an identical control panel.

3. Cambodia

1. These were topographic maps designed primarily for the use of troops on the ground. They showed cultural features (buildings, roads, settled areas), contour lines, and elevations. Because of their 1:50,000 scale, they were called "one-to-fifties," which was a

much larger scale than any aerial chart. It took more than one hundred of them to cover all of Cambodia. The overlaying grid system provided one kilometer squares, which were about 3/4-inch square. Using a six digit coordinate system, either the FAC or the ground commander could identify a square and a location within it to an accuracy of 100 meters or about 110 yards. For the time, that was considered excellent accuracy. Since the same maps were used by Seventh Air Force and by the Rustic Intelligence Section, there was no confusion over target selection. Throughout Southeast Asia, kilometers were the primary measurement of distance, although these could be converted to either statute miles or nautical miles. In military parlance, one kilometer was called a klick (about 0.62 statute miles) and short distances were specified in klicks.

2. In area, Cambodia is about 181,000 square kilometers or 70,000 square miles.

4. Bien Hoa Air Base—July 1970

1. As is true in many Asian countries, a person's family name is listed first. Kohn Om is the Americanized version of his Cambodian name, Om Kon.
2. Actually, the Vietnamese New Year (Tet) coincides with the Chinese New Year, which occurs sometime between late January and February. Missue still had a degree of immunity from being eaten.

5. The Night Rustics

1. The Saigon Combat Air Patrol mission (or "rocket watch" as it was called) was more political than practical. By keeping a combat aircraft constantly overhead, it helped promote a feeling of security to people on the ground. Actually, communist 122mm rockets were carried by hand and launched using portable launchers. They were undetectable from the air until they were fired. Then the FAC overhead could give Blue Chip about ten seconds of warning, which wasn't even enough to turn on the rocket sirens. Attacking the launch sites was useless. Within minutes the NVA or Viet Cong would be gone and there would be nothing to attack.
2. The tape transcript doesn't do justice to San Sok's eloquent words. Bob Harris uses this tape during speeches to civic clubs and high school classes. It gives the audience a new perspective on what the Rustics were doing and why they believed in it.
3. The standard-issue Air Force pilot's wristwatch had a "hack" feature that allowed the second hand to be stopped and started by pulling and pushing the winding stem. This allowed the watch to be hacked precisely to another watch or chronometer. In World War II movies, the bomber crews all hacked their watches at the end of the briefing. That really happened, but it was of no particular use over Cambodia. The hack feature, though, allowed the wristwatch to be used as a stopwatch.
4. The accuracy of air-delivered munitions (bombs, bullets, rockets, or napalm) depended on release angle, airspeed, altitude, and, to a great extent, the skills of the pilot. In those days, the munitions had no guidance system of their own and where they hit was essentially determined at the instant of release. Through testing, each type of munition had a circular error probable (CEP), which was an imaginary circle around the target that all munitions were expected to be within. This CEP plus the safe separation distance from unprotected friendly troops influenced both the FACs' selection of muni-

tions and the specific target location. Once the fighters dropped (or shot) their munitions, where they actually hit was called the circular error average or CEA. As part of the poststrike bomb damage assessment (BDA) the FAC would frequently give the fighters his estimate of their CEA, which, if all went well, would be less than the expected CEP for that weapon.

6. Communications, Intelligence, and the Rules of Engagement

1. The KY-28 Secure Voice system was essentially an electronic scrambler that scrambled UHF radio transmissions received by any radio that did not have the KY-28 equipment with the correct code installed. Both sending and receiving stations had to agree to "go secure" and turn on their Secure Voice systems as the quality of the transmissions was poor compared to the unscrambled transmissions. The code changed daily at midnight when all systems, both air and ground, had to have the new code inserted with a special key. This could not be done in-flight as the keys were never carried on the aircraft and the equipment was inaccessible. Without the key, the equipment was useless and of no value to the enemy. This is similar to the way the German Enigma code machine of World War II was rigged and defeating it was one of the British intelligence triumphs of the war. As it turned out, the Enigma machine could be improperly used, which gave the British clues as to the nature of the daily codes. The KY-28 did not have this deficiency.

2. Hotel call signs were a source of constant confusion. Three-digit call signs were assigned to individual commanders. Two-digit call signs went to major units. Subordinate units usually had a letter appended. A subordinate unit of Hotel 21 might be Hotel 21 Alpha or Hotel 21 Bravo. By August 1970, the Rustics had a list of more than sixty Hotel call signs that might or might not have been active.

3. The question of which enemy was present was difficult to resolve. In most cases, it was the North Vietnamese Army (NVA), a professionally trained and equipped military force. In some cases, it could have been the South Vietnamese Viet Cong, but it didn't seem likely that the VC would attempt to send an expeditionary force deep into Cambodia. The Cambodian communists, the Khmer Rouge, were still training their military forces in North Vietnam and were not considered a significant force at least through 1972. In 1973, they started to emerge, particularly in areas around Phnom Penh. By 1974, after the Rustics were deactivated, they were the dominant enemy force in Cambodia.

7. Chenla I

1. Weapons are usually designated by bore diameter. Caliber is an English (mostly American) measurement and is in inches. A .50 caliber machine gun has a bore of 1/2 inch. The rest of the world measures weapon bores in millimeters. The 12.7mm machine gun was manufactured in a number of different versions in Russia, China, and other communist bloc countries. It was patterned after the American .50 caliber gun and 12.7mm is almost exactly 1/2 inch. In combat, the enemy gun was frequently referred to as a ".51 cal. machine gun," but no one is sure where that designation came from. There is

no such weapon. If you round the millimeters-to-inches conversion factor (0.03937) and then round the answer, you can get .51. Throughout this book, enemy machine guns are referred to as 12.7mm guns, although they could have been captured American .50 cals.

2. Chandler, *The Tragedy of Cambodian History,* 207.

3. IFF stands for Identification, Friend or Foe and was an electronic device developed during World War II to allow radar identification of aircraft. A code setting is called a "squawk" and a code of 77 indicated an emergency and alerted the ground radar operator. Today, the same basic device is called a Transponder and is installed in all U.S. aircraft, both military and civil. It has a greater capability and the emergency squawk is now 7700.

4. OV-10 serial number 67-14626, the plane Jim Siebold and Walt Friedhofen were flying, is now on display among other special operations planes at Hurlburt Field, Florida. All OV-10 and O-2 FACs were trained at Hurlburt. Number 626 was flown in combat by many Rustics, including the author, and it always brought them home.

5. Becker, *When the War Was Over,* 131.

6. CBU stands for cluster bomb units. These were small bombs or bomblets that could be dropped from a dispenser mounted on a bomb rack or dropped in a bomb-shaped container that would split open as it fell and release the bomblets. The bomblets came in a wide variety of shapes, sizes, and weights and were generally used as wide-area anti-personnel weapons. Depending on the type, the detonation could be either instantaneous or delayed.

8. River Convoys

1. Under the current law, the United States could provide weapons and equipment to Cambodia but could not provide any assistance, instructions, or advice on how it should be used. See the foreword to this book, written by Mark Berent, Air Attaché, United States Embassy in Phnom Penh. The training that the Rustics provided the Cambodians at Bien Hoa and later at Ubon was arguably legal because it occurred outside Cambodia.

2. Deac, *Road to the Killing Fields,* 109.

3. The Navy flew the OV-10A, but did not use it as a Forward Air Control aircraft. Their OV-10s had an extra weapons station under each wing and usually carried 5-inch Zuni rockets. The aircraft were used for direct air support of the Navy operations on the rivers of the Mekong delta region.

4. *Stars and Stripes* is an Army newspaper printed wherever American troops are stationed and distributed free each day to all servicemen. It contains U.S. news, world news, and news of the specific area in which the troops are stationed. It also has the normal features found in any newspaper including sports news, a few comic strips, and a crossword puzzle. In Vietnam, it represented the only regular news from home and it was hugely popular. Although it was an Army publication, the Army exercised very little editorial control over it. *Stars and Stripes* subscribed to all the major wire services and published local area news under the same restrictions as other news media. If it was not

classified and they could verify it, they printed it. Their reporters were professionals and a large number of well-known journalists learned their trade on *Stars and Stripes*.

9. Chenla II

1. Etcheson, *The Rise and Demise of Democratic Kampuchea,* 111.
2. In August 1973, about the time all American air operations ceased in Southeast Asia, Colonel Oum was sent to the Cambodian Embassy in Bangkok, Thailand, as the Cambodian Defense Attaché.
3. Deac, *Road to the Killing Fields,* 114–15.
4. At the "debriefing," Lanny Trapp's story of his shoot-down was tape recorded.
5. The NVA in Cambodia seldom took prisoners and usually executed any that they captured. The Cambodian troops knew this.
6. At the time, it was rumored that Lon Nol was the "high official" being escorted.
7. *Stars and Stripes* almost certainly had one of their enterprising reporters in Phnom Penh and may have had one accompanying Lon Nol on his helicopter survey of the battle. They reported that Lon Nol had personally ordered the evacuation of Kompong Thma.

10. Ubon, Thailand

1. The U.S. Air Force operated from six Royal Thai Air Force bases in Thailand. This was classified until the late 1960s. By 1970, it was no longer secret and Thailand had become a regular overseas duty assignment for USAF personnel. Thailand was not directly involved in the conflict, but Thailand did keep an army unit in South Vietnam (as did many other countries) in support of the South Vietnamese and the United States. The Thai base was at Long Thanh North, a few miles east of Bien Hoa. The Nineteenth TASS kept O-2s and pilots there to support the Thai army. There was never any question about Thai support for United States efforts in Southeast Asia.

   The bases used in Thailand were Ubon (fighters, gunships, and the Rustics), Udorn (fighters and ABCCC aircraft), Takhli (fighters), Korat (fighters), Nakhon Phanom (special operations aircraft, fighters, and the OV-10 Nail FACs), and U Tapao (B-52 bombers and KC-135 tankers). Don Muang airport at Bangkok was used frequently by military aircraft, but it was not officially an Air Force base.
2. When the United States plans to station military personnel in another country, they first negotiate a Status of Forces Agreement, called a SOFA. The SOFA covers items such as how many personnel will be there, where they will be stationed, what rights and privileges they will have, which country's laws or procedures will apply if there is a crime or an accident, and so on. Although there are certain standard items covered in every SOFA, they are all slightly different as each item is negotiated separately with each country.
3. Language training for all U.S. military personnel was conducted at the Naval Post Graduate School at Monterey, California. Depending on the language, the training lasted about six months and was considered by many to be a very pleasant experience at a beautiful location.

11. No Rest for the Rustics

1. Steel Tiger was the name for both the operation and the area in the southern panhandle of Laos. Its purpose was the interdiction of supplies moving down the Ho Chi Minh trail from North Vietnam through Laos and Cambodia to South Vietnam.
2. The term "short round" is an old artillery term. In traditional battlefield employment, artillery was positioned behind front lines and fired over the heads of the frontline troops. Any round that fell short for any reason was called a "short round" and was assumed to have hit the friendly soldiers. In Vietnam, the Air Force adopted the term and used it to describe any situation where air-delivered munitions hit friendly forces.
3. John Schlight, *A War Too Long: The History of the USAF in Southeast Asia, 1961– 1975* (Washington, D.C.: Air Force History and Museums Program, 1966), 90.
4. Deac, *Road to the Killing Fields,* 142.
5. Stanley Karnow, *Vietnam: A History* (New York: Viking Press, 1983), 643–46.
6. The Nixon tape was provided by Mark Berent. He also provided it to John Clark Pratt who published it in *Vietnam Voices: Perspectives on the War Years 1941–1975* (Athens: University of Georgia Press, 1984).
7. In the OV-10, the parachutes were built into the ejection seats. The pilot wore a light-weight harness and was attached to the seat by a seat belt and two straps that came over his shoulders and fastened to two quick-release fittings (called Koch fittings) on his harness. In-flight, these straps served as the pilot's shoulder harness. After ejection, they became the main risers for his parachute.

12. The Final Rustic Missions

1. Chandler, *The Tragedy of Cambodian History,* 226–29
2. Becker, *When the War Was Over,* 156. Carl Berger, ed. *The United States Air Force in Southeast Asia 1961–1973: An Illustrated Account* (Washington, D.C.: Office of Air Force History, 1984) 147.

Epilogue

1. Becker, *When the War Was Over,* 160. After Saloth Sar defeated Lon Nol, he officially changed his name to his nom de guerre, Pol Pot.
2. Warren A. Trest, *Air Commando One: Heine Aderholt and America's Secret Air Wars* (Washington D.C.: Smithsonian Institution Press, 2000), 242.
3. Chandler, *The Tragedy of Cambodian History,* 232. Shawcross, *Sideshow,* 105.
4. Becker, *When the War Was Over,* 160.
5. Ralph Wetterhahn, *The Last Battle: The Mayaguez and the End of the Vietnam War* (New York: Carroll & Graf, 2001) provides a complete description of the Mayaguez incident.
6. See also Mark Berent's foreword to this book.

Bibliography

Becker, Elizabeth. *When the War Was Over: Cambodia and the Khmer Rouge Revolution.* New York: Public Affairs, Perseus Books Group, 1986; rev. 1998.

Berger, Carl, ed. *The United States Air Force in Southeast Asia, 1961–1973: An Illustrated Account.* Washington, D.C.: Office of Air Force History, 1984.

Chandler, David P. *The Tragedy of Cambodian History: Politics, War, and Revolution since 1945.* New Haven: Yale University Press, 1991.

Criddle, Joan D., and Teeda Butt Mam. *To Destroy You Is No Loss.* New York: Atlantic Monthly Press, 1987.

Deac, Wilford P. *Road to the Killing Fields: The Cambodian War of 1970–1975.* College Station: Texas A&M University Press, 1997.

Etcheson, Craig. *The Rise and Demise of Democratic Kampuchea.* Boulder, Colo.: Westview Press, 1984.

Hering, George C. *America's Longest War: The United States and Vietnam, 1960–1975,* 2nd ed. New York: McGraw-Hill, 1986.

Karnow, Stanley. *Vietnam: A History.* New York: Viking Press, 1983.

Pratt, John Clark, compiler. *Vietnam Voices: Perspectives on the War Years 1941–1975.* Athens: University of Georgia Press, 1984.

Ross, Russell R. *Cambodia: A Country Study.* Washington, D.C.: U.S. Government Printing Office, 1990.

Rowan, Roy. *The Four Days of Mayaguez.* New York: W. W. Norton & Company, 1975.

Schlight, John. *A War Too Long: The History of the USAF in Southeast Asia 1961–1975.* Washington, D.C.: Office of Air Force History, 1966.

Shawcross, William. *Sideshow: Kissinger, Nixon, and the Destruction of Cambodia.* New York: Simon and Schuster, 1981

Trest, Warren A. *Air Commando One: Heinie Aderholt and America's Secret Air Wars.* Washington, D.C.: Smithsonian Institution Press, 2000.

Wetterhahn, Ralph. *The Last Battle: The Mayaguez and the End of the Vietnam War.* New York: Carroll & Graf, 2001.

Index

Page numbers in *italics* refer to illustrations